P9-CJE-869

The Mushroom Manual

the
mushroom
manual

Tops! Complete for College Class;
Simple for You and Me

by Lorentz C. Pearson

 NATUREGRAPH PUBLISHERS

Library of Congress Cataloging in Publication Data

Pearson, Lorentz C., 1924—
   The Mushroom Manual

   Includes index.
   1. Mushrooms--United States. 2. Mushrooms--United
States--Identification. I. Title.
QK617.P38 1986   589.2'223'0973   86-21847
ISBN 0-87961-160-X
ISBN 0-87961-161-8 (pbk.)

A morel (*Morchella conica*). *Morchella* are among the most choice
of all mushrooms and are included in the Foolproof Four. ➤

Books for a better world

Naturegraph Publishers, Inc.
P.O. Box 1075
Happy Camp, CA 96039
U.S.A.

contents

preface

How many species of fleshy fungi, or mushrooms, are there? No one seems to know. Part of the problem lies in basic definitions: How leathery can a fungus be and still be called fleshy? How small can it be and still be called a mushroom? My best estimate is that the mushroom population consists of at least 7,000 species in North America and 15,000, possibly twice that many, worldwide. An authority on western mushrooms has suggested that there may be three to four thousand species of fleshy fungi, including "conks" or bracket fungi, in Idaho alone, where I do most of my mushroom hunting. These figures include hundreds of borderline species—species fleshy enough to be considered mushrooms by some people, or large enough that someone might pick one up to eat. Obviously, no one person can know all of the mushrooms, nor can one book describe them all.

Compared to other plants, mushrooms tend to be cosmopolitan. While there are few species of flowering plants native to all of the continents, or even to both North America and Europe, hundreds of mushrooms are world-wide in distribution, natives to both Europe and America.

The mushroom flora of Europe is better known than that of any other part of the world. Numerous beautifully illustrated books describe clearly Europe's 2,000 or more species. The flora of the eastern United States is also well known and amply described in many books. The very diverse mushroom flora of the American West, on the other hand, is not well-known or well-documented. Almost every North American genus is found in the Intermountain and Pacific Coast region and, in many of the genera, there are species found only in the West. This rich diversity is surprising to many people, because the West lacks the "lushness" of the East when it comes to fungus vegetation.

This book includes the common western species, in addition to the widely distributed cosmopolitan species also found in the East, making it valuable to both westerners and easterners. Edibility ratings, based on a variety of published sources, as well as on my own taste testing experience, are provided for each species.

Because the emphasis in this book is on mushroom eating, its pleasures and its dangers, an attempt has been made to include as many North American mushrooms known or suspected of being poisonous to man as possible. Species that are difficult to differentiate from each other have purposely been lumped together under the species name of the most poisonous member of the group. I feel this is the most satisfactory way to prevent possible poisonings among mushroom hunters; though I realize it is certainly not satisfactory for the serious student of taxonomy.

I have long been convinced that the best way to enjoy the pleasures of eating wild plants, while avoiding the unpleasantries of being poisoned, is to learn a few species well and then gradually expand one's knowledge. Chapter Two describes in considerable detail the characteristics of four groups of mushrooms that are so distinctive and easily identified that I call them the "foolproof four." This group of four expands to 15 in Chapter Four by the addition of another 70 edible species that are also easily identified if the precautions spelled out in the chapter are carefully observed. Other species of edible mushrooms are suggested in the keys in Chapter Five, but amateurs are advised to collect these only for purposes other than eating—unless comparisons are made with pictures and detailed descriptions from several sources, and until they have gained considerable experience in mushroom keying.

The keys in Chapter Five have been tested by my students over a period of several years and have been modified, improved, and added to from time to time. I appreciate the input of these many students. I also value the helpful suggestions of friends and colleagues with whom I have hunted mushrooms, especially Gordon

Hoagland, Earl Hansen, Peter Jeppsen, Ed Williams, and my own daughters and sons-in-law. Finally, I acknowledge the help received from teachers, like Clyde Christensen at Minnesota, and the authors of many popular and scientific books on mushrooms without which I never could have begun to study the mushrooms of Idaho or any other area.

Throughout the book, edibility is indicated by these symbols (daggers for poisonous and stars for edible species):

†   – poisonous species

††   – deadly poisonous species

○   – undesirable but non-poisonous, or untested species

†○☆ – poisonous, but edible after parboiling

☆   – edible species

☆☆   – good species

☆☆☆ – choice species

○(☆) – species that are edible but not recommended; easily confused with poisonous species

☆/†   – species ordinarily edible but poisonous under some conditions (*e.g.*, if consumed with alcohol or eaten raw)

☆/†○ – species probably edible but conflicting reports suggest caution

Spore prints of mushrooms representing the most commonly encountered spore print colors. Beginning at the top and going clockwise: BLACK, free or seceeding gills *(Panaeolus retirugis)*, BLACK, deliquesced *(Coprinus comatus)*, BROWN *(Bolbitius vitellinus)*, OCHRACEOUS BROWN *(Inocybe geophylla)*, PURPLISH BROWN *(Stropharia coronilla)*, WHITE *(Pleurotus ostreatus)*, BLACK, adnate gills *(Panaeolus campanulatus)*. In the center, SMOKY *(Gomphidius maculatus)* and PALE BUFF *(Amanita velosa)*. On the color strip at the bottom of the illustration from left to right, BLACK, SMOKY, BROWN, PURPLISH BROWN, CINNAMON BROWN (TERRA COTTA), OCHRACEOUS BROWN, OCHRE, PINK, PALE BUFF, WHITE. ➡

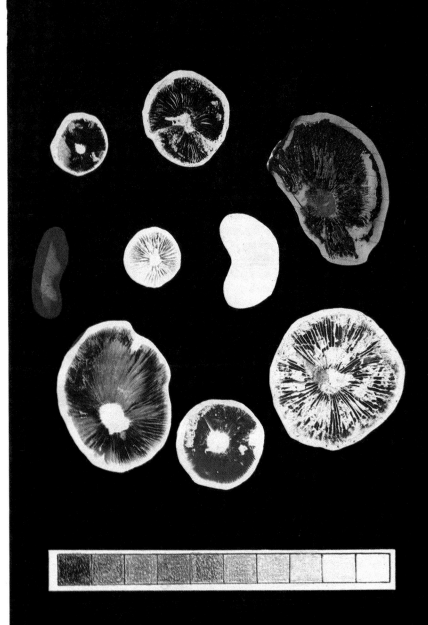

what to look for

More and more people are turning to mushroom hunting as a family activity. Long recognized in Europe and in the East as a pleasant way to foster family togetherness while adding choice gourmet items to the pantry shelves, mushroom hunting is fast becoming a family activity in the West as well. Compared to hunting deer and elk, searching for mushrooms is a quiet and peaceful way of obtaining food while enjoying the beauty of the Great Outdoors. Nevertheless, there are dangers in mushroom hunting, often more subtle than those of other outdoor activities. In the spring of 1979, for example, a young man was poisoned in eastern Idaho by eating the false morel. Every year poisonings occur in the United States or Europe from the Amanitas. What all of these poisonings have in common is that the victim failed to observe certain basic rules which every mushroom collector must obey. These basic rules will be spelled out in this chapter.

The safest place to hunt mushrooms is the grocery store. But anyone who has enjoyed the delectable and variable flavors of wild mushrooms is not likely to be satisfied with store mushrooms for long. Fortunately, there are precautions that can be taken to make hunting wild mushrooms safe.

the first rule. NEVER eat a mushroom unless you are 100 percent positive of its identification! The same rule applies to berries, wild herbs, and other foods. There are two groups of mushrooms that are especially easy to recognize, which every mushroom hunter must know. I call them the "foolproof four" and the "fatal five." After you know these two groups, you can go on to other groups. But never lose sight of the first rule of mushroom hunting: NEVER EAT A MUSHROOM UNLESS YOU ARE 100 PERCENT POSITIVE OF ITS IDENTIFICATION!

mushrooms and toadstools. The term "toadstool" is often used by people to suggest a useless or poisonous mushroom. Many people think there are two kinds of fleshy fungi, mushrooms and toadstools, just as there are two kinds of seed plants, angiosperms and gymnosperms. In the minds of these people, the mushrooms are edible and the toadstools are not, and they think mushroom gatherers know how to tell them apart just as foresters can distinquish between softwoods (or gymnosperms) and hardwoods (or angiosperms). Such is not the case, however. The term "toadstool" has no botanical meaning except as the common name of *Amanita muscaria,* also known as the "fly agaric." There are thousands of species of mushrooms, just as there are hundreds of species of berries, belonging to many families. For example, some berries belong to the rose family, while others to the saxifrage, heath and other families. Within every family of flowering plants there may be edible species, and those that are not; species that have never been tested for edibility, and some that are poisonous. In the nightshade family, the tomato, eggplant, and pepper are edible and wholesome, while the bella donna and the black nightshade are deadly poisonous. In the parsley family, the carrot, celery, dill, and parsnip are all edible while the water hemlock is very poisonous. Yet the water hemlock resembles the parsnip enough that people are frequently fooled and eat it, and bella donna berries could easily be confused with the delicious wonder berries which make such good pies. So it is with mushrooms: Within each family there may be both poisonous species and edible species, and the only way to tell them apart is to recognize the individual species.

Over the years, many superstitions have been associated with mushrooms. Some of these are amusing and harmless, such as the story of the fairy rings which show us the magic of where the fairies had danced in the early morning dew (Fig. 1). But some are dangerous: These have

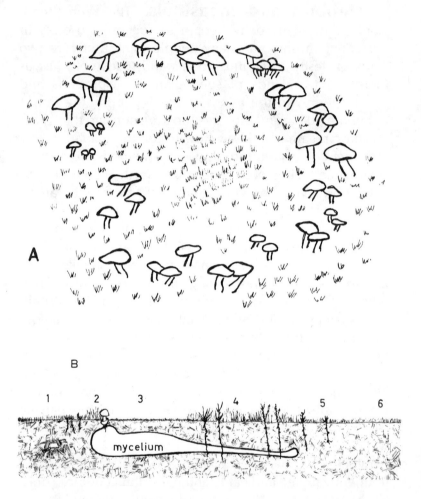

Fig. 1. Fairy ring. **A.** Fairy ring of *Agaricus* sp. in lawn; **B.** Cross-section through a fairy ring: (1) normal growth in lawn where mycelium has not yet reached, (2) zone of stimulated growth just behind apex of mycelium where the sporocarps appear, (3) vegetation stunted and yellow as a result of competition with mycelium for nitrates and other minerals, (4) zone of stimulated vegetation growth where mycelium is decomposing and releasing minerals, (5) zone of normal growth underlain by senescent mycelium, (6) center of circle where spores germinated and mycelial growth first took place.

to do with the identification of "toadstools" by simple characteristics. According to one "old wives' tale" it is possible to identify a poisonous mushroom because it will turn a silver spoon black. It is not known how many lives have been lost because of that superstition. Mushrooms which contain large quantities of methionine, cysteine, or other sulfur-containing compounds may turn silver black under certain conditions, whether they are poisonous or not, and there are many poisons which contain no sulfur at all. According to another false rule, poisonous mushrooms have white spores and edible mushrooms have pink, brown, or black spores. Among the deadly poisonous mushrooms may be mentioned the white spored *Amanitas*, the pink spored *Entolomas* and the brown spored *Galerinas*; other poisonous mushrooms have these and other colors in their spores, depending largely on their genetic (or taxonomic) relationships. Another old wives' tale explains that edible mushrooms are easily peeled and poisonous mushrooms cannot be peeled. This superstition is also worthless and dangerous. Some people believe that "the worms can tell," that wormy mushrooms are not poisonous, so they eat non-wormy specimens of species which have worms in them. Humans and worms have different metabolic pathways and things that are poisonous to people are not necessarily poisonous to worms, or fly maggots, that feed on mushrooms. This superstition, worse than worthless, could easily lead to illness or death.

basic rules for successful mushroom hunting.

A few species of mushrooms are deadly poisonous, just as poisonous as the plants Bella Donna, water hemlock, larkspur, loco week, or deathcamas. Other species are slightly poisonous or unwholesome in varying degrees, like ephedera, horsetail, and some other vascular plants. Then there are several hundred species which have been tested and found to be edible and safe, sometimes delicious. But the largest group of mushrooms are the thousands of species which have never been tested. Some of these are obviously undesirable, even if they should turn out to be nonpoisonous; some are woody, others have a foul odor, others are so small it would take dozens to make a taste-size morsel. Every year new species are tested for edibility and we are gradually discovering new treats for the table. Taste testing unknown species of mushrooms, however, is a risky past-time and should never be undertaken until one is completely familiar with the "fatal five" as well as with the rules of the taste testing game.

Although there are not many species of poisonous mushrooms, compared to non-poisonous species, to eat wild mushrooms indiscriminately is like playing Russian roulette. Even the most experienced mushroom hunter makes mistakes in identification at times, but this is not serious if the rules stressed in this chapter, especially rule number one, are observed. Here are the basic rules for successful mushroom hunting and eating.

1. Never eat a mushroom unless you are positive of its identification.

2. Never make a pig of yourself; when eating a new mushroom (one you have never tried before), even one which you know is not poisonous, try only a small portion the first time. You may be allergic to some nonpoisonous mushrooms; many people are.

3. Never overestimate your ability to identify a mushroom when in a new locality; when collecting an old favorite in a new area, start out by trying only a small portion of it.

4. Before eating any wild mushrooms, learn **totally** the characteristics of a small number of edible species and eat only these. Do not fret over your lack of ability to identify every fungus you see or worry about throwing away nice looking specimens; if you are not 100 percent certain of your identification, throw the specimen away or donate it to a herbarium—but **do not eat it.**

5. Know the terms used to describe mushroom characteristics, learn the kind of variations that can be expected to occur in these characteristics, and know the Fatal Five and their characteristics perfectly.

6. Never eat wild mushrooms raw.

7. Do not eat mushrooms with unpleasant or peppery flavors, or mushrooms that are worm-eaten or show signs of decomposition.

Rule no. 3 is of special importance to westerners. Books on mushroom identification have been written largely for eastern and European species. There are more species of mushrooms in the West than in the East, and there are also many more untested species. Furthermore, western ecotypes of eastern species are often different from eastern ecotypes of the same species, and this causes confusion. In the West, where mountains and deserts isolate populations from each other, there seems to be more variation within species than in the East. There is evidence that species hybrids are more common in the West, probably because there are more species per genus in many areas. Characteristics that vary the most are those which amateurs tend to note and remember best, namely, color and size; be especially alert to possible misidentification if the keys or pictures you are using are based largely on differences in the size and color of the sporocarps.

Commit these seven rules to memory and always observe them. There are exceptions to rules 6 and 7, but these are few and will be spelled out in the recipes you use. Never make an exception to the first four rules.

what are mushrooms? The mushroom we eat (or avoid because of its poison) is the "fruit" of a colorless plant called a fungus. Most of the mushroom species are members of the class Basidiomyceteae or club fungi, and a few are members of the Ascomyceteae or sac fungi, but the two classes are closely related to each other. Fossils of sac fungi have been discovered in rocks that are almost 350 million years old. At that time great forests covered much of the land surface of the earth, and red algae were forming reefs in the oceans. It is believed that the first sac fungi evolved from red seaweeds which were growing on the driftwood washed into the ocean from the forests. At the present time there are about 70,000 species of sac fungi and 20,000 species of club fungi all descended from these first marine ascomycetes. Some sac fungi still live on debris in the ocean, others are saprophytes living on leaf litter and rotting logs on land, and still others are parasites living on crops and other flowering plants. Likewise, some club fungi are saprophytes or parasites on seed plants. Many club fungi form symbiotic relationships with seed plants, acquiring their food from the plant while aiding it to obtain water and/or mineral nutrients. These particular fungi, known as the mycorrhizal fungi, grow on or in the roots of trees or other plants where they alter the morphology of the roots in a characteristic way. Many trees cannot survive without their mycorrhizal partner.

Every plant consists of two parts, the vegetative portion (such as the roots, trunks, branches, and leaves of a tree) which produces the food necessary for life and carries on the main part of the metabolic activities of the plant, and the reproductive part (such as the flowers and fruit of an angiosperm). The vegetative part of a fungus is called the mycelium, a collection of hyphae, or tiny thread-like "roots," growing wherever there is adequate organic matter in the soil. Unlike green plants it cannot manufacture sugars from carbon dioxide and water; but it can manufacture amino acids and other foods from the nitrogen and other minerals in the soil. The mycelium contains powerful enzymes which can break down the complex and very stable organic compounds, like lignin and cellulose, into sugars and other simple organic substances. These simple compounds are used as the energy source for all the metabolic activities of the mycelial cells including growth, reproduction, amino acid synthesis, fat synthesis, etc. The reproductive part of many fungi, a large, fleshy spore fruit, occurs when two mycelia of the same species contact each other and form a zygote from which the tissues of the fruit develop. It is this spore fruit which we call the mushroom.

Mushroom-producing mycelia, extensive perennial fungi, grow at the interface between leaf litter and the inorganic layer of the soil. The mycelium, developing from a single spore, often develops in a very symmetrical manner from its point of origin, and requires abundant nitrogen in the form of ammonia or nitrates for its best growth. At this stage, it competes with other plants for these minerals, and often the grass surrounding the mycelium will be yellowish in color indicative of not enough nitrogen. At times, the yellow zone will form an almost perfect circle on a lawn or meadow; such circles are termed "fairy rings" (Fig. 1). Following a rain, spore fruits, i.e. mushrooms, will pop up through the soil and litter along the edge of these yellowed rings, one mushroom for each fairy that participated in the dance the night before.

Each spore fruit produces millions of tiny spores. In most mushrooms, these are formed on the gills, the blade-like structures on the underside of the mushroom cap. In other species, they are formed inside pores or on other structures of the spore fruit. These spores may then be carried by natural means, such as the wind, to new locations where, if favorable to their growth, they will germinate into new mycelia.

how to identify mushrooms.

Some mushrooms are so distinctive that they can be quickly and easily recognized any time they are encountered. Others are difficult to recognize because their characteristics either are variable or else blend with characteristics of other species. Even the most experienced mushroom hunters occasionally make mistakes in identifying mushrooms.

Little harm is done in misidentifying a mushroom as long as you faithfully obey rules 1 and 2 and never eat a mushroom unless you are 100 percent positive of its identification, and never over-indulge when eating a new mushroom. If you know the Fatal Five so well that you never mistake one of them for an edible species, it is possible to taste mushrooms you have slight doubts about providing you taste only a very small portion. However, even a piece of one of the Fatal Five the size of a pea could lead to serious illness or possibly death, as some of the most potent poisons known to man exist in fungi.

The "typical" mushroom consists of cap and stem with gills on the undersurface of the cap. In some species the gills are attached to the stem; in other species the gills are free from the stem. Stems are stringy and tough, similar to cartilage, in some mushrooms, but rather fleshy, consisting of what appear to be short fibers, in other species. Some species have rather distinctive markings on the stems that aid in their identification. Likewise, the form of the cap (varying from parasol-shaped to flat, even some resembling small funnels) helps in identification. The structures that are especially useful in mushroom identification are illustrated in Fig. 2.

Collecting and identifying mushrooms is a satisfying activity in and of itself, whether one intends to eat the mushrooms or not. The mushroom hunter who can readily identify every sporo-

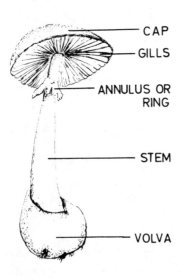

CAP

GILLS

ANNULUS OR RING

STEM

VOLVA

Fig. 2. Sporocarp, or spore fruit, of a typical gill mushroom (*Amanita phalloides*) showing major morphological structures.

carp he sees is rare indeed. Even the professional mycologist may spend hours trying to identify some of the specimens he collects, and the most experienced hunter-gourmet will throw away more fruits than he eats. Enjoy the challenge of "keying out" new species without worrying about their edibility. The keys presented in Chapter Five and the genus and family descriptions in Chapter Six will help you to identify unknown species. When you do find a few choice specimens for your table, consider that a bonus. Of course, after your have gained experience, you will know where and when to go each year to find favorites, as most mushrooms are perennials that send up their sporocarps year after year in the same place when weather conditions and soil moisture are just right.

As you collect, pay special attention to the characteristics in the following list, then wrap the mushrooms in wax paper (not plastic), either individually or in small groups of the same kind. **Never** put two species of mushroom in the same wrapping. Place the wrapped mushrooms carefully in a wicker basket or similar rigid container. Wherever possible, collect three sporocarps of each species; at your first opportunity, use one of them for a spore print (see page 33).

Careful attention should be paid to the following characteristics:

1. Presence or absence of an annulus (or ring).

2. Presence or absence of a volva (or cup).

3. Consistency of stem, whether fleshy-fibrous or cartilaginous.

4. Attachment of the stem to the cap.

5. Attachment of the gills to the stem.

6. Waxiness of the gills.

7. Nature of spore-producing structures other than gills, when present.

8. Shape of the cap.

9. Cap margin, whether entire, scalloped, eroded, inrolled, etc.

10. Color of cap and stem.

11. Spore color.

12. Presence or absence of minute hairs, scales, or glands, on cap or stem.

special characteristics of spore fruits. A

universal veil often encloses the spore fruit when it first pushes through the soil of the forest floor, lawn or meadow; in addition, a partial veil may cover the gills. As the spore fruit grows the veils rupture; sometimes they leave bits of tissue on the surface of the cap or on the stem (Fig. 3). If the universal veil leaves a ring of tissue, or bits of tissue, on the stem, it is called a volva. The volva, often beneath the surface of the soil, may go unnoticed unless the mushroom is collected carefully. If the partial veil leaves a ring of tissue around the stem, it is called a ring or annulus. The annulus may be located high on the stem, low on the stem, or centrally. In the *Amanitas*, both ring and volva are usually present; in *Agaricus, Galerina,* and many other genera only a ring will be present; in many other genera neither volva nor ring will be present. Sometimes the annulus is a prominent membranous ring, sometimes it is a fringe of hairs, at other times it is reduced to an obscure scale-like marking or series of markings.

Stem consistency varies considerably among mushrooms. In the *Russulas* and *Lactarii*, the stem is brittle, almost like chalk; in the *Galerinas* and *Panaeolus*, the stem is thin and tough, like cartilage; in *Agaricus, Amanita,* and *Boletus*, the stem remains succulent and fleshy-fibrous. In some cases, as in *Russula* and *Lactarius*, the consistency of the stem alone is usually enough to identify the mushroom to genus, but stem length, cap color, and other characteristics are needed to distinguish among the species of the genus.

The attachment of the stem to the cap and the gills to the stem are also important characteristics. In most mushrooms, the stem connects right at the center of the

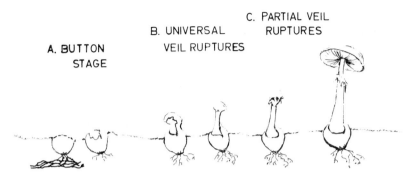

Fig. 3. Stages of development in a single sporocarp of a mushroom having both universal and partial veils: **A.** The sporocarp, enclosed in a universal veil, pushes up through the soil; **B.** The universal veil ruptures leaving a volva or "death cup," at or below the soil surface and scattered "warts" on the cap; **C.** The partial veil ruptures leaving a ring or annulus on the stem and, in some species, a "cortina" on the margin of the cap.

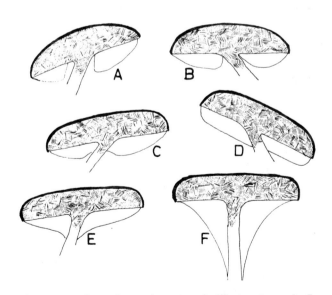

Fig. 4. Different modes of attachment of gills to stem: **A.** Free, **B.** Adnexed or notched, **C.** Emarginate, **D.** Adnate or square, **E.** Arcuate, **F.** Decurrent.

cap. In many species, however, the stem fastens off-center, and in some species it is attached to the edge of the cap. Some mushrooms have no stems and the cap joins directly to the stump or trunk or other substrate on which the mushroom grows, usually at the margin of the cap.

The gills may be completely free of the stem or they may be attached to it in various ways, some of which are illustrated in Fig. 4. Every mushroom student should know the difference between free, adnexed, adnate, and decurrent attachments. It is sometimes difficult to distinguish between free and adnexed; however, if the gills are free, it should be possible to see a ring of cap tissue between the stem and the gills, and if the gills are adnexed, the remnants of the gills should be visible at the top of the stem when it is removed.

In a few genera, the gills are waxy, which is a very useful characteristic for identification. Holding the cap upside down, press firmly on the gills and rub. If wax is present, the gills will not only feel waxy, but wax will adhere to the fingers. In checking for this characteristic be certain it is the gills themselves that are waxy as many mushrooms, including commercial ones, contain slimy material on the caps that may fool you into thinking they are waxy. To distinguish between "waxy" and "merely moist" gills, practice on the non-waxy commercial mushroom, *Agaricus.*

Most gill mushrooms have gills with entire edges (i.e. without notches or indentations), but in a few species the gills have sawtooth edges or wavy edges. This characteristic is uncommon, making it useful in identifying species.

Not all mushrooms have gills. In the Ascomyceteae, or sac fungi, the spores appear on the upper surface of the spore fruit. The spore fruit of the fleshy sac fungi is always an apothecium, but apothecia vary considerably in general form. The "typical" apothecium is a plate-like or cup-like structure as shown in Fig. 5. Sometimes the plate is completely flattened like a disk, and at other times, it

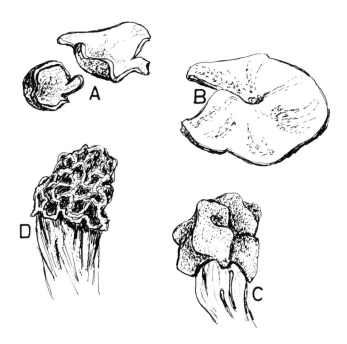

Fig. 5. Variations in the form of apothecia of sac fungi (Ascomyceteae): **A.** Cup-like in *Peziza repanda* (similar to *P. vesiculosa* but larger and growing on wood), **B.** Disk-like or slightly concave disk in *Discina ancilis,* **C.** Convex disk in *Helvella lacunosa,* **D.** Extremely convex disk with pits in *Morchella conica.*

reaches the extreme in flattening, becoming convex (Fig. 5, C, D).

In the Basidiomyceteae, or club fungi, a number of morphological types of spore fruits occur. In the chanterelles, coarse veins rather than gills occupy the undersurface of the spore fruits. In the *Clavarias,* or coral mushrooms, spores are borne on all surfaces of a many branched spore fruit. In the tooth fungi, tooth-like projections protrude from the undersurface of the cap and the spores reside on these. In the boletes, polypores, and their relatives, spores are produced inside tiny tubes which make up the undersurface of the cap. In the puffballs, there is no differentiation in the spore fruit, of special spore bearing tissue

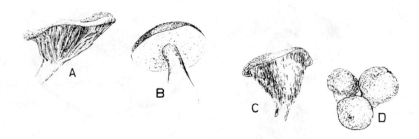

Fig. 6. Variations in the form of basidiocarps of club fungi (Basidiomyceteae): **A.** Dichotomously branched veins, with cross veins, in *Cantharellus cibarius;* **B.** Pores in *Boletus eastwoodii;* **C.** Teeth in *Hydnum repandum;* **D.** Internal spore production in *Lycoperdon perlatum.*

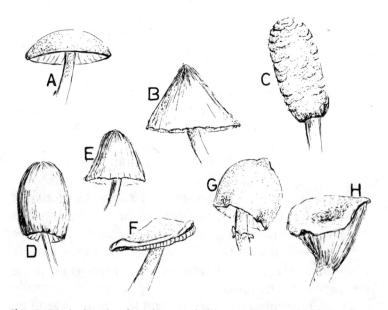

Fig. 7. Variation in the shape of the mushroom cap, or pileus: **A.** Convex, **B.** Conic, **C.** Narrowly parabolic, **D.** Broadly parabolic, **E.** Campanulate, **F.** Plane or flat, **G.** Mammillate or umbonate, **H.** Depressed (if depressed with an umbo or knob in the center, it is called umbillicate).

(or hymenium), except for a thin epidermis, which converts into spores as it matures. Some of the variations in basidiomycete spore-bearing surfaces are shown in Fig. 6.

The shape of the cap is often useful in identification, but tends to vary considerably within any species. Some of the terms given typical mushroom shapes (see Fig. 7) are geometrical, such as convex, conic parabolic, and plane, while others are botanical and zoological. Campanulate means shaped like a bell; mammillate bears resemblance to a breast with an umbo or nipple at the apex of the fruit; depressed indicates having the margins of the fruit higher than the center; umbilicate is depressed like a navel with an umbo in the center. During maturation, slightly convex fruits often become depressed and funnel-shaped; a spore fruit that emerges with a convex cap may become plane-shaped; or the young fruit may be mammilate, but gradually become convex.

In most mushrooms, the margin of the cap is either entire or smooth (Fig. 8A) or slightly wavy or undulating (Fig. 8B). The margin may also be crisped (Fig. 8C), crenate (8D), or appendiculate (ragged with bits of cap tissue hanging from the margin as in 8E). In some species there will be striations visible on the upper surface of the cap near the margin, and some species have very distinct striations running the entire length of the cap from margin to apex (Fig. 8F). Some of these characteristics disappear or become more pronounced as the mushroom matures so they are not to be totally relied upon in identifying species.

The color of the cap tends to vary considerably with its age, and also varies from one specimen to another, collected short distances apart from each other, within the species. Nevertheless, within relatively broad limits it may be a very useful characteristic in distinguishing the species within a genus. This is especially true in the genera *Russula, Boletus,* and *Clavaria.* Spore color, on the other hand, varies only slightly within species and is usually constant for entire genera. There are several ways to ascertain the color

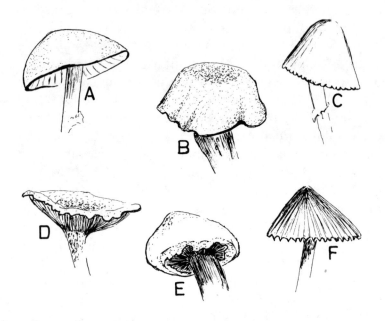

Fig. 8. Variation in mushroom cap margins: **A.** Entire or smooth, **B.** Undulating or slightly wavy, **C.** Crisped, **D.** Crenate, **E.** Appendiculate, **F.** Serrate with distinct striations on the cap surface.

of spores, but the most reliable and easiest way is to obtain a spore print.

Contrast versus uniformity in color of cap compared to stem is often more useful in identifying species than the specific colors of each. Often stem and cap are identical in color, but sometimes the base of the stem is darker (or lighter) than the upper part. Occasionally either the cap or the stem, or both, will change color when bruised or when the flesh is broken and exposed to air for two or three minutes. Your fingers, in some cases, will be stained by substances in the cap or stem. Watch very carefully for changes that occur in the color of the flesh when bruised or broken as a valuable aid in ascertaining certain species.

In many species, hairs cover the cap, the stem, or both.

These usually small hairs are easily seen with a hand lens. In other species, small or large scales cover part or all of the cap and/or stem. Note carefully their characteristics when present. Glands or glandlike markings occur on some species of mushroom; web-like remnants of the veils or net-like markings on the stems characterize other species.

obtaining a spore print. Probably the single most important characteristic of gill mushrooms, as far as identification is concerned, is the color of the spores. Spore color is frequently important in identifying boletes, coral fungi, tooth fungi, and chanterelles as well. The surest way of ascertaining spore color is with the aid of a spore print, and it is generally wise to prepare a spore print of every mushroom you collect at the earliest opportunity. Where several specimens of the same species are collected in the same locality, make it a simple routine to take one of the specimens and prepare from it a spore print, but be sure to label it and the rest of the collection in such a way that after the print has been obtained you know which species it goes with (see page 15).

To make a spore print cut (or break in species in which the cap and stem separate easily) the stem off just beneath the cap and place the cap, gill side down, on a piece of white paper. Over the cap, arrange a tumbler or any other vessel that will hold the air around it quiet and allow humidity to increase. If the cap is dry, a piece of wet cotton or tissue paper can be placed inside the tumbler—e.g., on the top of the cap. The spore print will usually be ready in an hour or two, although in some cases it takes several hours. To help see white prints, place the mushroom cap half on white and half on black paper; however, this is not essential. A microscope cover slip placed under the cap can aid in studying the size, shape, and markings of individual spores.

When the spore print is ready, the outline of the gills is readily visible. Some people make a practice of collecting spore prints of several species on a single piece of paper and mounting this under glass. A very attractive piece of artistic work can be obtained when the caps are arranged carefully.

At the time the mushrooms are collected, natural spore prints are sometimes present on leaves or other objects under the mushrooms. This is frequently the case when gregarious mushrooms are found and the upper ones have left prints on the upper surface of the caps beneath them. Observation of these natural spore prints can save time in making accurate identifications.

There are other ways of obtaining spore color information, but these should be resorted to only in cases when spore prints cannot be obtained. For example, in cold weather although not cold enough to freeze the caps, often mushrooms will not produce spore prints. About 70 or 80 percent of the time, the gills on mature mushrooms will be colored by the spores and spore color can be ascertained from gill color. This is not a recommended method, however, because the color of the gill will generally not authentically reflect spore color in young specimens and in many old specimens as well. Spores can be examined by removing a small piece of gill or pore tissue and examining it under a microscope; this requires more work than using spore prints and the colors are difficult to assess. For chilled mushrooms, this may be necessary, however, but keep in mind that the color of individual spores is much lighter than that of masses of spores; furthermore, reds and browns in masses of spores may appear yellow in individual spores. Sometimes spore deposits can be found on the stem of the mushroom and spore color recorded from these deposits.

Spore colors vary considerably with many shades of each basic color. For purposes of identification, five basic colors are generally recognized: White, pink, brown, purple-brown, and black. Pale yellow spores occur in some species and are included with white in most mushroom keys.

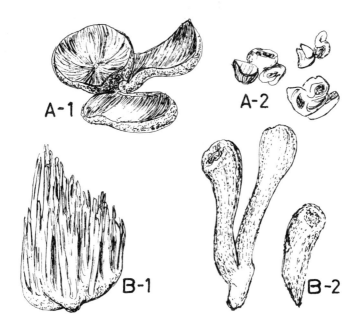

Fig. 9. Spore fruits of jelly fungi (A) and coral fungi (B): **A-1.** *Auricularia auricula* (also known as *Hirneola auricula-judae)*, **A-2.** *Tremella lutescens,* **B-1.** *Ramaria stricta,* **B-2.** *Clavaria borealis.*

major groups of mushrooms. On the basis of type
of spore fruit, fleshy fungi or mushrooms can be divided into eight major categories. (Fig. 2, 4, 5, 6, and 9):

1. Those with the hymenium, or sporogenous tissue, on the upper surface of the cap, the Ascomyceteae.

2. Those with gills on the undersurface of the cap.

3. Those with dichotomously branched veins on the undersurface of the cap.

4. Those with teeth on the undersurface of the cap.

5. Those with pores on the undersurface of the cap.

6. Those consisting of branched stems bearing spores; without caps.

7. Those with the spores filling the entire inner cavity;

8. The jelly fungi with disk-like "caps" and no stems.

The agarics or gill mushrooms can be further divided into four categories: (1) Those with gills free from the stems; (2) Those with attached gills and fleshy-fibrous, thick stems; (3) Those with attached gills and spindly, usually tough and cartilaginous stems; and (4) Those with stems attached off center, or to the margin, or attached by the margin to the substrate without stems. Likewise, the pore fungi can be divided into two groups: (1) Those with a thick, succulent pore layer which usually grow on the soil or in rich organic matter, and (2) Those with a thin drier pore layer which usually grow on trees, stumps, and rotting logs.

Each of the four sub-groups of gill fungi can be further divided into five groups (three in the case of sub-group 4) on the basis of spore color. The sub-groupings of fleshy fungi will be further discussed in Chapter Five.

the foolproof four

In the early 1970's research on the "chunk hypothesis" demonstrated that we can organize, remember, and make use of information best if it is divided into chunks of manageable size. The "magic number" associated with rapid recall and efficient memorization is five. Applied to mushroom hunting, the chunk hypothesis suggests that we will be successful as amateur mushroom hunters if we select not more than five species of mushrooms and learn these well before going on to additional types. That means that when we go hunting we will save, to begin with, only those four or five species we have chosen and throw everything else away—or use them only for practice in getting acquainted with mushroom morphology. As suitable for a beginning point, the four mushrooms Clyde Christensen describes as "the foolproof four" in his book, *Common Edible Mushrooms* (University of Minnesota Press, 1947) are the ones examined in this chapter.

Fortunately, there are a few species of mushrooms that are not only safe to eat, but are rather common, and not closely related to any of the poisonous varieties. They are so distinctive and different from all other mushrooms that there is no danger of misidentification. Among these are Christensen's "foolproof four":

1. The morels
2. The puffballs
3. The shaggy mane
4. The sulfur polypore

Not only are the foolproof four common, safe, and easily identified, they are among the most delicious of all mushrooms. Learn their characteristics well. If you never learn any other wild mushrooms, you will still know more than most of your friends. The rewards you receive from knowing these four well justifies the time it will take to learn them.

morels. The morels have a brittle, hollow stem and pitted cap, and are so distinctive in appearance that once you have seen even a picture of one, you cannot mistake them. There are several species, all of them edible and some of them among the choicest of all mushrooms. There are no poisonous morels; the false morels are easily recognized by the wrinkled rather than the pitted cap.

Morels should never be eaten raw. There are reports of indigestion or possibly mild poisoning from people who have eaten the dark colored (black) morels raw. The substance causing the problem has been chemically isolated and studied; it is water soluble and volatile, evaporating at about 65° C. When fried or boiled, the toxic substance soon evaporates and problems of indigestion have been solved.

Morchella esculenta is the most delicious of the morels, and many people rate it the best of all mushrooms (Fig. 10). Its flavor is distinctly different from that of other fungi, and even children who do not like commercial mushrooms often enjoy this morel. A favorite way of preparing it is to split the stems and end of the cap and stuff the hollow cap with small pieces of cooked chicken, tie the split stem together, roll in egg and then bread crumbs, and bake or fry in butter. Another popular method of preparing it is simply to slice and fry in butter (not margarine) with onions.

The morels are most abundant in early spring near melting snow, but they have been found in the mountains of eastern Idaho in late July. They sometimes come up

Fig. 10. *Morchella esculenta,* the common morel.

abundantly after a forest or brush fire. In the Plains States and the West they are sometimes abundant on the cottonwood covered islands and bottomlands adjacent to the rivers. For unexplainable reasons, they may be very abundant year after year along a stretch of the river a half mile or so in length and absent for the next stretch of several miles; then after years of heavy production, they will disappear for a year or two even from the places where they have been abundant. During the spring rains of April or May, depending on latitude, they will suddenly appear, be abundant for two or three weeks, and then disappear again until the following year.

puffballs. The puffballs have a thin skin and soft, white interior which turns to spores upon maturity. When ripe, they cannot be mistaken for anything else; however, they are no longer edible when ripe. When immature and edible, some simple precautions must be taken to ensure that they really are puffballs; these are so simple that there is no reason for anyone ever being poisoned by eating what he thought was a puffball but in reality was not.

Morphologically, there are two groups of puffballs, those with a pore at the top of the sporocarp through which the spores escape, and those in which the upper surface of the sporocarp crumbles away at maturity freeing the spores (Fig. 11). The latter group are often referred to in Europe as "egg mushrooms" rather than puffballs. Children enjoy playing with the "true" puffballs, for the slightest amount of pressure on the sides of the sporocarp provides a bellows actions, sending up a cloud of brown or black "smoke" through the tiny pore.

Puffballs are common throughout summer and fall on drier sites, often occurring alongside trails and forest roads near openings. They sometimes are found in the desert under sagebrush. They always grow above ground, on the surface of soil or litter, or on logs. They vary greatly in size, but all are white, roughly spherical to pear shape, and usually ornamented with little spines, bumps, or a mosaic of cracks or wrinkles. Some of the gregarious species are typically pullet egg size and smaller, but so many sporocarps are produced close together that despite their smallness they can be profitably collected for the table. Other puffballs are extremely large. A Ricks College student found three specimens of *Calvatia gigantea* a few years ago on a little island in the Snake River at St. Anthony, two of them about 40 cm. in diameter and the third about twice that size. Had he known what a prize he had, he could have fed his whole dormitory with his find. Unfortunately, he allowed them to lie around until they began to spoil before donating them to the Biology Department, believing all the while that they were "toadstools" and therefore worthless.

There are no poisonous puffballs, but there are two groups of mushrooms which are occasionally mistaken for puffballs. To avoid all danger, always take the simple

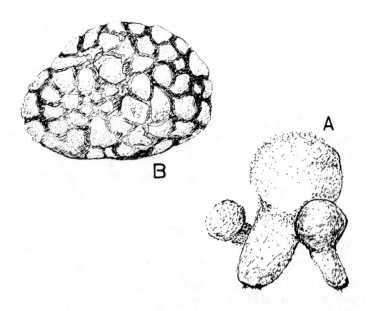

Fig. 11. Puffballs: **A.** *Calvatia subsculpta,* **B.** *Lycoperdon perlatum.*

precaution of cutting puffballs lengthwise and examining the nature of the spore-bearing tissue before eating. If there is any differentiation of tissues, such as the beginnings of stem and gills, the specimen in hand is probably not a puffball. In puff-balls, the gleba, or interior tissue, is uni-formly white and spongy in nature, later turning yellow and then brown. Some puffballs do have a rudimentary stem at the base of the sporo-carp, but any puffball-like mushroom, in which an embryonic stem extends from base to apex through the center of the dissected sporocarp, or in which embryonic gills occur, is definitely not a puffball (Fig. 12).

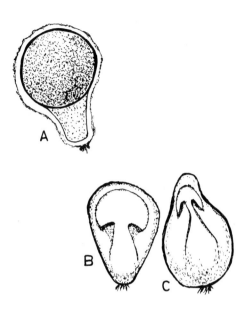

Fig. 12. Longitudinal sections of mushroom "buttons": **A.** Edible stage of puffball, *Lycoperdon candida.* **B.** Button stage of *Agaricus campestris,* **C.** Button stage of *Amanita phalloides.*

The two groups of fleshy fungi which might be mistaken for puffballs are (1) the root truffle, *Scleroderma aurantium,* a poisonous species which grows underground but superficially resembles a puffball; it has a tough, leathery skin and very compact flesh which soon turns black, rather than yellow as in the puffballs; and (2) many mushrooms look like puffballs when they are very young or in the "button stage"; however, when the buttons of gill and pore mushrooms are cut lengthwise, the beginnings of the cap and stem are visible whereas puffballs have a uniformly white texture throughout. There are people who have eaten *Amanita muscaria* buttons, thinking they were puffballs; if they had cut into the mushrooms before eating them they could not have made such a painful and frightening mistake.

Puffballs are relatively mild flavored and can be used raw in salads, sliced and fried in butter, or diced and stewed. They should be eaten before the interior begins to change color. However, some people claim that even the slightly discolored ones have a good flavor; they are certainly harmless. A favorite way to prepare them is to slice thin, dip in a beaten egg and then in cracker crumbs, and fry. Puffballs are very high in protein, about 25 percent, and are reported to have a good balance of amino acids.

the shaggy mane. The shaggy mane, *Coprinus comatus*, is the only gill mushroom among the Foolproof Four. It belongs to a group of mushrooms called "inky caps" because the gills and spores dissolve at maturity into a black inky mass. Like other inky caps, the shaggy mane will not keep more than a few hours after picking, even in a refrigerator, unless the sporocarps are placed in a bottle of cold water. If kept in cold water, they will keep two or three days. Most inky caps are edible; none of the common species are poisonous except that *Coprinus atramentarius* in combination with alcohol causes severe digestive disturbances and hallucinations in some people. The shaggy mane is the best of the inky caps and is so easy to recognize that once you have seen a specimen or a picture of one, you can readily identify it (Fig. 13). Note the cylindrical to narrowly parabolic cap with large, brown-tipped tufts of hair-like scales covering the white surface. Young specimens usually have a narrow, loose ring, or annulus, around the upper part of the stem which soon disappears. The only mushroom which even superficially resembles a shaggy mane is *Podaxis pistillaris*, a tropical desert species which bears its spores inside the sporocarp like a puffball. *Podaxis* caps never open up nor do their "gills" deliquesce.

Like other species of *Coprinus*, the gills of the shaggy mane are pinkish when young, but turn black and then deliquesce—turn into a liquid or gelatinous mass—at maturity. The gills of *Panaeolus*, a genus of black-gilled mushrooms, many of them poisonous, which are sometimes mistaken for *Coprinus*, do not change from pink to black and do not liquify.

Fig. 13. The shaggy mane, *Coprinus comatus.* The middle sporocarp is in the best stage for eating; the one on the right is over-mature and the gills are deliquescing.

Shaggy manes are reported to be among the most easily digested of all mushrooms. They can be steamed for five minutes and served with butter and cream or they can be fried or baked. For a delicious treat when shaggy manes are abundant, butter a baking dish, put in a layer of mushrooms then bread crumbs and grated cheese, season with salt and pepper and add another layer of mushrooms. This can be repeated two or three times, adding butter to the top layer, and baking for 15 to 20 minutes.

The shaggy mane is a fall mushroom, very common in lawns and among the shrubs bordering lawns wherever decaying roots or stumps of hardwoods occur. After several black locust trees were removed and replaced with asphalt to extend a parking lot on the Ricks College campus, shaggy manes popped up through the blacktop every fall for three or four years. They usually appear in large numbers, often right next to or even in the middle of a road, both at very high elevations where there may still be snowbanks close by, and in the valleys near where the desert replaces the forest.

Shaggy manes are large enough that there is no problem obtaining plenty for a full recipe of your favorite mushroom dish. Most specimens are 10 to 15 cm. high, but occasionally a giant one weighing a quarter of a kilogram will be found. Large shaggy manes may be over-mature with gills starting to deliquesce at the margins; if so, remove the margin and use the rest of the fruit.

the sulfur polypore.

The sulfur polypore, *Polyporus sulphureus,* belongs to a group of wood-inhabiting fungi called shelf fungi. Most polypores, commonly called "conks," are very tough and woody and therefore not suitable for human consumption. Some conks are foul smelling; apparently none are poisonous, but have the nutritional value of a two-by-four. The sulfur polypore, however, is not only edible and nutritious, it is delicious. It grows on rotten logs and standing trees, both dead and alive, especially oak, but also on ash, alder, willow, and fruit trees, among others. Shelf fungi are readily recognized by the pores on the undersurface of shelf-like, stemless caps; the sulfur polypore is fleshy and typically has many overlapping, fan-shaped shelves coming out of a fallen log in the form of a rosette. The upper surface is usually orange and the undersurface sulfur yellow, but the shelves of some varieties are orange brown in color. It is a common mushroom in Europe, in the eastern United States, and in some areas of the West Coast, but is not common in the Intermountain Region (Fig. 14).

Polyporus sulphureus fruits from midsummer on, and is especially common in the fall, occurring wherever old decaying trees are abundant. Clumps of the overlapping, fan-shaped shelves sometimes weigh several kilograms and extend from point of attachment to the trunk or log 10 to 25 cm. outward. The margins are fleshy and cheese-like in consistency, but the bases may be somewhat woody. The typical yellow variety has been found in northern Idaho near Moscow, but the brownish orange variety is more common in the Island Park area of eastern Idaho near Lower Mesa Falls. Once a location has been spotted where sulfur poly-pores fruit, you can keep coming back to the same place for several years confident of finding them again.

Fig. 14. The sulfur polypore, *Polyporus sulphureus.*

The sulfur polypore, also called "chicken-of-the-woods," is delicious sliced and fried in butter or dipped in egg and breadcrumbs and fried. When breaded, it is reported to resemble chicken breast in flavor. A favorite recipe in Sweden is to soak in salted water for a few hours, rinse in cold water, then cook with dill for 20 minutes in the same way crayfish are cooked. It is then served cold, either by itself or in a salad, as a substitute for crayfish or lobster.

The Foolproof Four are by no means the only mushrooms that can be collected safely, but they are among the very choicest of all edible fungi. They are common enough that you can usually find them, and are among the easiest to recognize. Once the characteristics of the Foolproof Four have been mastered, you can go on to other groups.

the fatal five

In terms of total species, few mushrooms are poisonous. The odds are much better than 50–50 that a mushroom picked up at random in the forest or meadow will be safe, and probably edible. In fact, the odds are better than the 5 to 1 that Russian roulette players face. But why play Russian roulette, for there are many mushrooms that are poisonous. At least ten species can be called "deadly poisonous" in the sense that eating even a small piece will likely lead to death. An additional four species are known to have caused death in humans under certain circumstances. These 14 species belong to five taxonomic groups that are referred to here as the "Fatal Five." There are other poisonous mushrooms that should be carefully avoided; in fact, there are others strongly suspected of causing deaths, but the Fatal Five are so dangerous that every mushroom hunter should know their characteristics "by heart" and be able to recognize them any time or place. In the following discussion they are presented in order of toxicity beginning with the most dangerous.

The seven deadliest species belong to two complexes or groups of closely related species: the *Amanita phalloides* complex with five species and the *Entoloma lividum* complex with two. Potentially almost as dangerous as these are three species in the *Galerina venenata* complex. Over the years, deaths have also been attributed to eating large quantities of any one of three species belonging to the *Amanita muscaria* complex. Finally, the delicious and much sought after *Gyromitra esculenta*, or false morel, has caused deaths in rare cases.

Do not suppose that these are the only poisonous mushrooms on the face of the earth; they are merely the only **deadly** poisonous mushrooms that we know anything about. There are thousands of species of mushrooms that have never been tested for toxicity; some of them may be not only poisonous, but deadly poisonous. Mushroom toxins are among the most poisonous substances known to man; it is not wise to experiment with new species unless some very important precautions are taken.

mushroom toxins. The poisons found in mushrooms can be classified into four main groups based on how they affect the body physiologically. These are (1) protoplasmic poisons, (2) gastrointestinal irritants, (3) nerve poisons, and (4) disulfiram type poisons. Each of these groups can be subdivided into additional groups. Most of the deadly poisonous mushrooms contain toxins of the first two types; the poisons in the *Amanita muscaria* complex are of the third type.

Amanitin and gyromitrin are the two poisons referred to as protoplasmic toxins. They are slow-acting poisons which dissolve cell membranes and thus destroy tissues. Amanitin, which is also know as phallin, is the toxic principle in mushrooms of the *Amanita phalloides* and the *Galerina venenata* complexes. After eating a mushroom containing amanitin, ten to twenty hours may pass before any symptoms are noted; then, very abruptly, violent vomiting and diarrhea will begin. This may continue for two or three days until death results. If the amount of amanitin taken was very small, however, the symptoms will cease and the patient seems to be recovering. After a day or two, he may suffer a relapse as a result of progressive injury to his liver, kidneys, heart, or skeletal muscles and, in at least 50 percent of the cases, will die after two to five days.

Any person suspected of having eaten a mushroom containing amanitin should be immediately hospitalized, preferably long before any symptoms develop. The stomach, of course, should be emptied. If possible, hemodialysis should be used. Maintenance of electrolyte and fluid balance is crucial. Experimentation in Europe with thioctic acid suggests that it may prove to be effective as an antidote; an antiphallin serum has been reported to be effective in France, but has not been available in the United States.

Amanitin is one of a group of toxins known as tox-albumins. Other tox-albumins are the venom of rattlesnakes and the toxin which destroys tissues in cholera and diphtheria patients.

Gyromitrin is similar in its mode of action to amanitin but is less toxic. It is relatively abundant in some strains of *Gyromitra esculenta* and occurs in small amounts in other species of *Gyromitra* and *Helvella* and possibly in the black morels. Gyromitrin is a water soluble, volatile substance and can be removed from the false morel and other mushrooms by parboiling. In parboiling, the mushroom is boiled in water in an uncovered container for at least 5 minutes and the water thrown away. The mushroom can then be rinsed in cold water and used in omelettes, casseroles, etc., or fried.

Note that parboiling will **not** remove amanitin! Do not parboil any of the *Amanita phalloides* group or *Galerina venetata* group thinking that you have removed any of the poison!

Compared to amanitin, it takes a relatively large dose of gyromitrin to be deadly. Furthermore, gyromitrin does not seem to be especially toxic to healthy people, but seems to be very poisonous to anyone who is sick or convalescing from a period of illness. One of the first symptoms of gyromitrin poisoning is loss of muscular coordination. Strains of *G. esculenta* vary considerably in gyromitrin content; European and eastern American strains tend to be high in gryomitrin and western strains apparently are low in content. Deaths have resulted as far west as Minnesota. At least one death has resulted from a child drinking the water in which *G. esculenta* was parboiled. It is essential that the parboiling water be immediately thrown away!

The second group of toxins are the gastro-intestinal irritants. There are several kinds of such irritants, most of them are fast acting and the symptoms terminate within a short period of time. In some cases, "sulfur burping" will be the only noticeable symptom, but the poisons found in the *Entoloma lividum* complex may be deadly; therefore, a physician should be called in all cases where a person is believed to have eaten a mushroom containing a serious gastro-intestinal irritant. After removal of the toxic material from the digestive tract, the patient should have plenty of rest and good diet.

Several species of mushrooms, in addition to those of the *Entoloma lividum* complex, are known to contain large quantities of dangerous gastro-intestinal irritants. People who have eaten *Boletus satanus,* or any of its close relatives, have become seriously ill to the point of requiring hospitalization. Species of *Hebeloma* and *Inocybe* have also produced serious illness. These mushrooms may be regarded as potential killers if eaten in relatively large quantity.

There are many kinds of nerve poisons; among the best known are muscarine, ibotenic acid, muscimol, psilocybin, psilocin, tricholomic acid, and pantherin. The active ingredients of the *Amanita muscaria* complex fungi are ibotenic acid and muscimol, two closely related and chemically interconvertible hallucinogenic compounds. These are fast acting toxins, producing their symptoms in most cases within 15 to 30 minutes. After a brief period of drowsiness, the patient becomes very excited, has pro-nounced muscle spasms, delirium, and hallucinations. This period of intoxication lasts for three to four hours and the patient then drops off into a deep sleep. Death is not common unless the patient has eaten large quantities of mushrooms. Chlorpromazine will reduce the intensity of the hallucination. During the depression stage that follows the hallucination stage, stimulants may be given, but alcohol should be avoided.

Psilocybin and psilocin also produce hallucinations. The first symptoms usually appear about an hour after eating mushrooms of the *Panaeolus, Psilocybe,* or *Conocybe* groups and include sensitivity to touch and changes in mood in addition to very vivid hallucinations. Recovery is ordinarily very rapid and complete.

Muscarine is found in mushrooms of the *Amanita muscaria* group, and in large quantities can be fatal. It is not as abundant in these mushrooms as muscimol and ibotenic acid are and it does not produce hallucinations. Symptoms include profuse sweating, irregular slow pulse, severe vomiting, and diarrhea.

The fourth group of toxins are the disulfiram-like constituents found in *Coprinus atramentarius* and a few other mushrooms. Like disulfiram, they produce symptoms only in the presence of alcohol. No one should consume any alcoholic beverage, including beer, within at least 48 hours either before or after eating mushrooms containing any of the toxins in this group. In the absense of alcohol, the mushrooms not only seem to be harmless but appear to be nutritious. Disulfiram is a harmless drug used in the treatment of alcoholics. Unlike disulfiram, the mushroom toxins seem to be highly variable in the way they affect different people and may not be harmless in the presence of alcohol.

amanita phalloides complex. These are the most dangerous of all mushrooms and have caused numerous deaths. Most mushroom hunters avoid all *Amanitas,* even though some, like *A. caesaria,* are regarded as among the most delicious. No amateur has any business collecting any *Amanita* for the table ! Probably not even experienced mushroom hunters should consider collecting edible *Amanitas* in western North America for eating. Every mushroom hunter should have the identifying characteristics of the Amanitas memorized perfectly and avoid all mushrooms resembling them at all !!

There are at least four species in the *Aminita phalloides* complex: *A. phalloides, A. bisporigera, A. verna,* and *A. virosa. A. mappa* is listed in some European references as a separate species and is reported to be just as poisonous as

A. verna and *A. virosa*. The active ingredient in all of these species is amanitin, also known as phallin. It is an extremely potent protoplasmic toxin and destroys the tissues of the liver, kidneys, and other organs. The content varies greatly from one specimen to another, but in general is most concentrated in *A. phalloides,* and almost as concentrated in *A. bisporigera.* Being a slow acting toxin, it is usually well distributed throughout the body by the time symptoms first appear. Stomach pumping has little value in saving the life of a person who has eaten any of these mushrooms if he waits until symptoms appear before seeking aid.

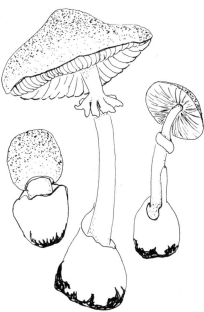

Amanita phalloides is illustrated in Fig. 2 and *A. virosa* in Fig. 15. Note the death cap or volva at the base of the stem and the ring high on the stem. Either of these features may be missing from a given specimen; rings often erode away on older specimens especially, and unless care is taken in digging up the base of the stem, the volva may be left in the ground.

The Amanitas may be recognized by the following combination of characteristics: (1) White gills which are free from the stem, (2) White spore print, (3) Untapered stem which is often swollen at the base, (4) Membranous ring which is rather high

Fig. 15. The deadly poisonous "destroying angel," *Amanita virosa. Amanita verna* is almost identical in appearance but the stem is smooth; *A. phalloides* is very similar but tends to be shorter, stockier, at least at the base, and usually has a greenish, more rounded, cap.

on the stem, and (5) Volva which typically forms a distinct cup-like structure, usually just beneath the soil surface. The *A. phalloides* complex are characterized further by white to lemon yellow or tan caps and smooth white stems. The different species can be distinguished from each other on the basis of cap color, ring and volva characteristics, and spore characteristics. *A. verna* has a wider volva than *A. phalloides* and is usually pure white. It is the most common species of the complex. In the Lake States it is often so abundant that one may count over a thousand specimens on a morning's walk. They are found growing singly or in groups of two or three in aspen groves and hazel brush. *A. phalloides* is characterized by a pungent odor similar to raw potatoes; though rare, it may be the most abundant member of the complex in southern Idaho. In northern Idaho and in the South, *A. bisporigera* is most abundant; it differs from other *Amanitas* in having only two spores per basidium instead of four. It is more slender than *A. verna* and *A. virosa,* and has a less well developed volva. *A. virosa* differs from *A. verna* in spore shape: Slightly elliptical vs. round. Some mycologists classify all four of these as varieties of *A. phalloides;* others regard only *A. bisporigera* as a distinct species.

Several western *Amanitas* have never been tested for toxicity. Some of them have adnexed rather than free gills and may lack ring, volva, or both. Do not experiment with any mushroom resembling an *Amanita* even if it does not have all the characteristics of the "typical" *Amanitas.*

Victims of *Amanita phalloides* poisoning all seem to testify that it is a tasty mushroom. Perhaps this is one reason that the mortality rate is so high for the *Amanitas*—it is estimated that more deaths have resulted from eating *Amanitas* than from all other poisonous mushrooms combined.

The common name usually applied to *A. phalloides* and *A. bisporigera* is "destroying angel"; *A. virosa* and *A. verna* are commonly known as "death cup."

entoloma lividum complex. Although the toxin is different and somewhat less powerful, its concentration is very high in a few mushrooms of the *Entoloma lividum* complex so that these mushrooms are potentially as dangerous as the *Amanitas.* However, they are not as common; furthermore, their foul odor after they have been picked for an hour or more undoubtedly discourages many mushroom hunters from trying them out.

Entoloma lividum and *Entoloma sinuatum,* also known as *Rhodophyllus lividus* and *R. sinuatus,* are both extremely poisonous. Other species of *Entoloma* are edible, but certainly not to be recommended simply because of the ever present danger of getting two species of the same genus confused. Neither species is common in North America, but *E. lividum* is relatively common in some parts of Europe.

E. lividum is readily recognized by (1) its pink spore print, (2) odor which resembles that of newly milled wheat, but soon changes to an unpleasant rancid odor, (3) hollow stem, and (4) finely adnexed, almost free gills. The distinctive odor alone will usually be sufficient for positive identification. Most mushroom hunters avoid eating any mushrooms with a milled cereal odor or with angular red or pink spores.

E. sinuatum is characterized by (1) pink spore print, (2) odor similar to that of burnt sugar, (3) solid stem, and (4) very broad, close, slightly adnexed gills. Whereas *E. lividum* is solitary or frequently in pairs or sets of three, *E. sinuatum* is gregarious, often with many stems arising from a common source. And while the odor of both is quite pleasant while fresh, that of *E. lividum* becomes very unpleasant with age. Both species have compact, white flesh and fleshy-fibrous stems which give them the appearance of good mushrooms for the table (Fig. 16).

Species of *Pluteus and Tricholoma* are the mushrooms most likely to be confused with *Entoloma* if good spore prints are obtained. *E. sinuatum* is easily distinguished by

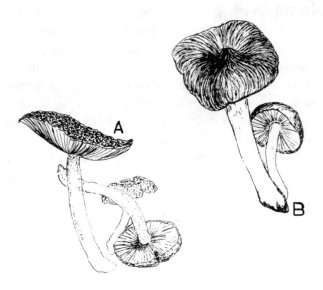

Fig. 16. Poisonous mushrooms with pink gills and reddish spores: **A.** *Entoloma lividum;* **B.** *Entoloma sinuatum.*

its gregarious habit, both species by gill color and/or gill attachment. *E. sinuatum* also resembles the "fried chicken mushroom," *Lyophyllum multiceps,* in many ways. Both grow in dense clusters, both have closely spaced white gills, and both have smooth, rounded caps. They differ in spore color and gill attachment: *L. multiceps* has white spores and adnate to slightly decurrent gills. The spores of *L. multiceps* are round, whereas *Entoloma* spores are angular. It is recommended that you always check spore shape before eating *L. multiceps;* do not rely on spore color alone.

· The silky entoloma, *E. sericeum,* is one of several edible species of *Entoloma.* It is considerably more common than either of the poisonous species and is probably more common, at least in the West, than any of the other members of this genus. Like *E. lividum,* it smells like newly milled grain. Because *E. lividum* is **deadly** poisonous and the two species are difficult to tell apart, it is recommended that *E. sericeum* and all other mushrooms having red, angular spores and adnexed gills be completely avoided as far as eating, or even taste testing, is concerned.

Two species of questionable reputation possibly contain the same toxin that the *Entolomas* contain. *Paxillus involutus* is reported to be a nice tasting mushroom and is eaten cooked, raw, and pickled by many people, apparently without any ill effects. Nevertheless, raw *P. involutus* is suspected of having caused at least one death. *Naematoloma fasciculare* is accidentally eaten at times, in spite of its unpleasant bitter flavor, by those who think they have colected *N. capnoides*, usually without any adverse effects. It too, is suspected of having caused deaths. In both cases, the deaths were of children or elderly people. *P. involutus* has brown spores; *N. fasciculare* has purple spores.*Naematoloma* is similar in general appearance to *Entoloma* except for the spore print, but *Paxillus* is quite different looking (Fig. 43). Both genera should be regarded as dangerous and care taken in choosing species for eating from either genus.

galerina venenata complex. The *Galerinas* are small

mushrooms, sometimes common in lawns, with parasol-like habit and cinnamon brown caps, gills, and stems. They are so small that it would take a very large number to make a meal and are therefore generally ignored by mycophagists. This is very fortunate, because some of the species contain the same toxin, amanitin or phallin, that is found in the *Amanita phalloides* group.

Galerina, Crepidotus, Gymnopilus, Pholiota, Rozites, Inocybe, Hebeloma, and *Cortinarius* are the most common genera belonging to the family Cortinariaceae. The family is characterized by spores colored some shade of brown, and gills attached to the stem. Many of the species have the spider-web-like fibrous veil, or cortina, which gives the family its name. Most species are saprophytes on wood, humus, or soil, or else form mycorrhizal associations with roots; none of them is found on dung. There are many poisonous species in the family: The *Galerinas* have group 1 toxins, *Hebeloma* has group 2 toxins, and *Inocybe* has group 3 toxins. *Cortinarius, Gymnopilus,* and *Crepidotus* species are poorly known as far as toxin nature is concerned, but the latter two have mostly tasteless or bitter species. Even though there are some excellent eating species in the genera *Rozites, Pholiota,* and *Cortinarius,* it is strongly recommended that no taste testing of species in this family be conducted except by professionals who have at their disposal the latest chemical methods to aid them in detection of amanitin and other toxins. It is also recommended that the amateur take very special care in identifying species belonging to any of these genera before eating them, even if he has done so before.

Fig. 17. Deadly poisonous LBM's: **A.** *Galerina venenata;* **B.** *Galerina autumnalis.*

In 1912, C.H. Peck reported a case of poisoning by *Galerina autumnalis* in which two children in New York died. Recently, Daniel Stuntz has reported a near fatal poisoning of a Portland, Oregon couple who ate *G. venenata* they found growing in their lawn. *G. marginata* is also poisonous, containing the same toxin as the other two species. Two other species of *Galerina, G. cerina* and *G. paludosa,* are common on moss, but are not known to be poisonous. *G. paludosa,* common in sphagnum bogs in Idaho, Washington, and Oregon, is easily distinguished from the other *Galerinas* by its ecological preferences and its distinctive mammillate cap. Even though it has not been reported to be poisonous, and though amanitin has not been isolated from it, do not experiment with this or any other species of *Galerina!*

G. autumnalis, also known as *Pholiota autumnalis,* is the most common of the poisonous mushrooms in this group. It is widely distributed throughout North America and Europe on well-decayed conifer and hardwood logs, occurring mostly in the fall, but sometimes in early spring. *G. venenata* is reported to be a rare species limited to the Northwest, west of the Cascade Mountains. There are unconfirmed reports, however, of *G. venenata* from lawns in parts of Idaho; if these are accurate, it is a much more widely distributed species than formerly believed. *G. marginata* is the least common of the three species and apparently does not occur in the West.

amanita muscaria complex. The *Amanitas* are relatively large, fleshy, attractive mushrooms of forested areas which look as though they ought to be edible and delicious. The odor is pleasant, and the taste is reported to be agreeable. Until *Amanita phalloides* and *A. bisporigera* were discovered in the West quite recently, *A. pantherina* was reported to be the most poisonous of the western mushrooms. *A. muscaria,* being the most common of the Amanitas, has been responsible for most cases of mushroom

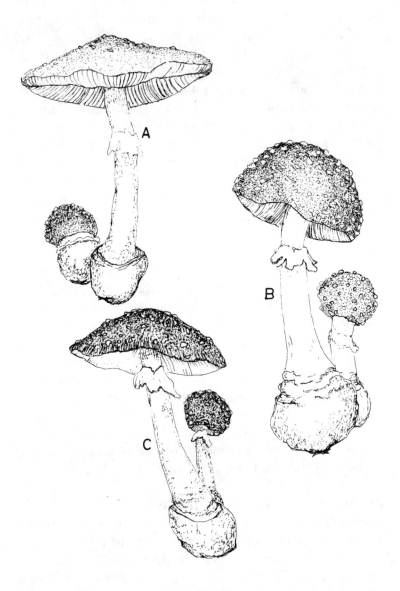

Fig. 18. The *Amanita muscaria* complex: **A.** *Amanita pantherina;*
B. *Amanita muscaria,* the fly agaric or common toadstool;
C. *Amanita umbrina,* a rare species, potentially deadly in relatively
small amounts.

poisoning in the West, in the East, and in Europe. Both of these species contain nerve poisons (type 3); both have caused deaths, but relatively large amounts of toxin are necessary if the poisons are to be fatal. Large quantities of toxin may be obtained by either of two ways: The mushroom eater may make a pig of himself and eat dozens or (in some recorded cases of fatal poisoning) even hundreds of mushrooms, or the victim may by chance obtain one or a few mushrooms with an unusually large amount of toxin present. *A. pantherina* specimens often have very large amounts of toxin present and are therefore especially dangerous. In either case, the symptoms come on rapidly and death is slow and painful.

Amanita pantherina, A. muscaria, and *A. umbrina* resemble other Amanitas in their general characteristics: (1) white gills which are free from the stem, (2) white spore print, (3) untapered stem which is often swollen at the base, (4) membranous ring situated centrally to high on the stem, and (5) volva which forms either a well developed cup or a series of scale-like rings at the base of the stem. These species usually have patches of scale-like tissue on the upper surface of the cap which are remnants of the universal veil and which give them the spotted appearance for which they are noted. *A. muscaria* "typically" has a bright orange cap with white patches, making it one of the most attractive mushrooms there is. Specimens collected in Idaho and other intermountain states however, are often almost white, instead of orange—but they are just as poisonous as the more "typical" specimens of the Pacific Northwest, Europe, and eastern United States. *A. umbrina* is brown with white patches. *A. pantherina* has a gray-brown to dingy-yellow cap with white leopard spots; intermountain area specimens, however, may be almost white. The spotting of the cap and the collar-like rather than cup-like volva distinguish these species from the *A. phalloides* complex of species (Fig. 18).

Spore color, spore morphology and biochemistry,

features of gill attachment, stem characteristics, and general cap morphology are more reliable characteristics in mushroom identification than color of the cap, gill, and stalk. General cap morphology is more variable than the other features listed. As pointed out in the previous paragraph, inter-mountain specimens of *A muscaria* and *A. pantherina* are lighter in color, as a rule, than West Coast and East Coast specimens. This can create problems with those who rely heavily on sporocarp color for identification. In Europe and in eastern North America, *Amanita silvicola* is easily distinguished from other white amanitas, like *A. virosa,* because it has a much shorter stalk and very poorly developed volva and annulus. Thus it resembles *A. pantherina* in size, stockiness, and to some extent, annulus and volva characteristics. Mushroom hunters used to collecting and eating *A. silvicola* in the East or in Europe have collected, eaten, and suffered severe poisoning from *A. pantherina* when they first encountered it in the intermountain area.

Unlike the toxins in the *A. phalloides* complex, those in the *A. muscaria* complex are fast acting and symptoms generally appear within 15 to 30 minutes after ingesting the mushrooms. The first symptoms are from the muscimol-ibotenic acid compounds: The victim becomes drowsy first, and then hallucinations and general intoxication-like behavior follow. At the drowsiness stage, and even at the intoxication stage, there is still time to help the victim by pumping the stomach, giving emetics, enemas, etc. Medical aid should be sought and the patient must be given plenty of bed rest and proper food for several days. Muscarine is also present in these mushrooms, but the concentration is much lower than that of muscimol and ibotenic acid; it is also more slowly absorbed and there-fore more readily removed by stomach emptying treat-ments. It is also more likely to cause death than are the other toxins present in these mushrooms.

The nerve toxins that occur in the *Amanita muscaria*

group of mushrooms are water soluble and can be removed from the spore fruits by parboiling. Bengt Cortin gives the following directions for *A. muscaria*—the directions must be followed to the finest detail! He does not recommend parboiling of *A. pantherina*, although it would *probably* be effective. **Never** parboil any mushroom of the *A. phalloides* complex—it will not remove their poisons!

To render *Amanita muscaria* safe to eat: (1) carefully peel the cap, removing every bit of the pellis or rind, as most of the muscarine is concentrated there; (2) cut into relatively small bits; (3) place the bits in boiling water and boil for exactly five minutes; (4) discard the water, and boil again in fresh, boiling water for an additional five minutes; (5) discard the water and prepare the mushroom in the usual way. The mushroom is edible but certainly not a choice one. If you make a mistake and choose a mushroom of the *A. phalloides* group instead of *A. muscaria*, amanitin will still be present and the mushroom as toxic as though you had eaten it fresh.

A. pantherina possibly contains toxins not found in *A. muscaria*. Pantherin, a chemical of unknown composition but probably similar to muscarin, had been reported in this species. Regard *A. pantherina* as potentially as dangerous as *A. virosa* and *A. verna* in the *A. phalloides* complex, and do not even taste test very small pieces of it.

Although there are several species of edible *Amanitas*, the variation within each species is so great, especially in the intermountain region where mushrooms are poorly known, that it seems very foolhardy for anyone, especially an amateur, to try any, or even to experiment with what appears to be a safe *Amanita*.

gyromitra esculenta.
The false morel is the most enigmatic of all mushrooms. It is one of the choicest mushrooms as far as flavor is concerned and seems to be completely harmless to most people. There are verified reports of deaths due to this species, however. Deaths

have occurred where individuals (1) ate large quantities of the mushroom, (2) ate the mushroom raw in relatively large quantities, and/or (3) were recovering from serious illness or were rundown and weak.

The toxin present in *Gyromitra esculenta* and some of its close relatives is a water soluble, volatile compound named gyromitrin, having a boiling point of 65° C and a tendency to form bonds with other organic compounds in the presence of heat. Parboiling will remove the toxin, but the conditions are even more exacting than for the removal of *Amanita muscaria* toxins.

To render *Gyromitra esculenta* safe to eat, follow these directions **exactly:** (1) remove dirt and debris and cut the mushroom into relatively small (bite-sized) pieces; (2) rinse in fresh water; (3) place in boiling water and boil for exactly four minutes, no more and no less; (4) pour off the water; (5) rinse in cold water.

Bengt Cortin stresses the necessity of getting rid of the water the mushroom was cooked in. In 1936 a Swedish child died from drinking the water used to parboil *G. esculenta* which had been poured into a tumbler instead of down the drain.

Even when the false morel is parboiled, it should not be eaten in large quantities. If not parboiled, it can probably be eaten safely if consumed very sparingly. In either case, do not eat another false morel for at least 48 hours.

Although serious poisonings and even deaths have resulted from eating *G. esculenta* in Europe and in the East, there has never been a case of mushroom poisoning reported in the West from eating cooked *G. esculenta* and only one case from eating a very large quantity of the raw mushrooms. At the present time we can only speculate as to the reason for this. The following hypotheses have been suggested: (1) western races or ecotypes of *G. esculenta* contain much less toxin than Eastern races; (2) in the West, the people who usually eat false morels are fishermen, hunters, and other outdoors people who are probably in better health; in the East, mushroom gathering is often a family outing activity and everyone, even those who are convalescing and therefore more sensitive to the toxin, take part in the eating of the mushrooms; (3) Westerners are not the avid mushroom hunters and wild mushroom eaters that Easterners are and therefore eat only a small amount of the mushroom, whereas Easterners tend more toward the "gourmet type" and prepare special mushroom dishes that are the center of the meal; (4) Westerners don't know how to care for wild mushrooms when they collect them; Easterners know that the proper way to care for newly collected mushrooms is to wipe them gently with a damp cloth but never wash them, whereas Westerners dump them in the sink, wash them as they would wash the Monday laundry, and then put them in the frying pan soaking wet. In the process of frying the water soluble

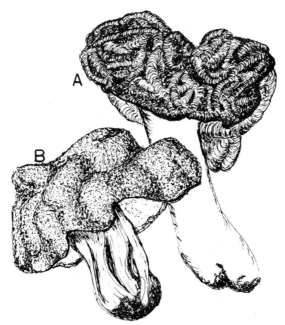

Fig. 19. False morels: **A.** *Gyromitra esculenta,* the common false morel or calf's brain mushroom; **B.** *Helvella californica,* a saddle fungus.

gyromitrin is boiled off and the mushrooms are as safe as though they had been parboiled. At the present time, it seems most likely that hypotheses (1) and (3) are the reason for no poisonings in the West to date. As new strains are introduced from other areas and as Westerners become more conscious of the food value of mushrooms, we may expect poisonings in the West to increase.

Gyromitra is readily recognized by the brain-like convolutions or wrinkles of the upper surface of the apothecium. *Helvella,* which in some taxonomic treatments includes *Gyromitra,* has a smooth upper surface; the upper surface of the apothecium of *Morchella* is pitted. *Verpa* sporocarps are conical and either smooth to slightly wrinkled, like *Gyromitra* and *Helvella,* or longitudinally ridged with partial cross ridges which give them the appearance, more or less, of conical *Morchellas.* These four genera have the sporocarps borne on stalks; *Underwoodia* is similar to *Verpa* but has no stem.

The wrinkles, or convolutions, on the cap of *Gyromitra esculenta* are very close together giving the sporocarp the appearance of a calf's brain, and hence the common name: Calf's brain fungus (Fig. 19). The cap is almost globose in contrast to other fleshy ascomycetes, like the *Verpa* spp., which have elongated sporocarps.

misc. causes of mushroom poisoning. In addition to actual poisons in mushrooms, the mycophagist needs to be aware of two other conditions that can cause trouble: (1) allergies and (2) nitrogenous toxins ("ptomaines") resulting from bacterial decomposition of mushroom proteins. To guard against allergies, always taste test a new mushroom (new to you, that is) even though you know it is nonpoisonous. To guard against the second type of poisoning, never eat worm infested, overmature or rotting specimens. In some cases only the lower stem may be worm infested and can be cut away, but often if there are worms in any part of the mushroom, they will be found

throughout when carefully examined. Avoid eating any portion of a mushroom having tell-tale pinholes even if visible worms are not present.

The worms that infest mushrooms are mostly the larvae of beetles or of flies. Beetle larvae have been shown to be just as nourishing as either mushrooms or beef, perhaps more so; the problem, however, is that bacteria digest the broken cells adjacent to the worm holes, resulting in very toxic nitrogenous compounds accumulating, and these poisons can cause severe sickness.

beyond the basic nine

While the Foolproof Four are among the choicest of all mushrooms, in addition to being easy to identify and relatively common, there are other mushrooms that are as good. One of the chief advantages of knowing and collecting wild mushrooms is that there are so many different flavors of which the eater of cultivated mushrooms alone is never aware. Even among the Foolproof Four, the diversity of flavors is considerable: The very mild flavor of puffballs, the chickenbreast flavor of the sulfur polypores, and the distinctive and rather "unmushroom-like" flavors of the morels and shaggy manes. Add to this the variability in flavor of the chanterelles, the fried chicken mushroom, the beefsteak mushroom, the oyster mushroom, the boletes, angel wings, and champignons; and the gasteronomic possibilities of the wild mushrooms become apparent.

However, before going beyond the Foolproof Four, it is good to become well acquainted with them, and it is essential to know the Fatal Five. With the mushrooms described in this chapter, mistakes are more likely, and one may end up with a case of poisoning unless great care is taken. The Foolproof Four and the Fatal Five make up what I call the Basic Nine—know them well before going on to more difficult species.

Probably the surest mushrooms to recognize beyond the Foolproof Four are the boletes. Many boletes are choice in flavor and usually very common. Their biggest drawback is that the choicest species often seem to be wormy. After the boletes, the scaly lentinus, the oyster and angel wing mushrooms, the champignons, and the inky caps are logical choices for the novice to form a close acquaintanceship with since they are all quite common, good tasting, and easy to identify if a certain amount of care is taken. The *Russulas,* milky caps, chanterelles, tooth fungi, and coral fungi are also relatively easy groups with which to work. Before going on to more difficult groups, it will be well to take a good hard look at some of the other poisonous mushrooms.

boletes or fleshy pore mushrooms. Some of the choicest of all species of mushrooms are found in the genus *Boletus*. There are some poisonous boletes, however, especially the appropriately named *Boletus satanus*, that one must guard carefully against. In the West, there are a few species of *Boletus* and several species of the closely related and often very similar genus *Suillus* that have never been tested for edibility. Keys are based on published descriptions of known species; a new species may seem to fit the key and the student thinks he has properly identified the specimen when in reality he has not. Therefore, there is always some risk associated with collecting table mushrooms in a territory as poorly studied botanically as the Intermountain Area.

The fleshy pore mushrooms are all included in the family Boletaceae which is closely related to the gill mushrooms. Superficially, they resemble the Polyporaceae more than their gilled relatives, but they differ from them in a number of ways: (1) The pore layer is thin and tough in the polypores, succulent and fleshy in the boletes; (2) the pore layer is easily separated from the rest of the cap in the boletes, but not in the polypores; (3) The boletes usually have a distinct stem and cap and grow on the soil while the polypores are typically "shelf fungi" growing on logs and stumps without stems; (4) Most polypore fruits are perennial with at least the older tissues becoming very woody while the fruits of boletes persist for only a few days and are not woody; (5) pores are often microscopic in the polypores but they are always visible to the naked eye in the boletes; and (6) most polypores have white or very pale spore prints while the spores of boletes are yellow to brown or darker in color.

"Lumpers" classify most members of the Boletaceae in

two genera, *Boletus* and *Suillus;* "splitters," on the other hand, have created a dozen or more additional genus names such as *Boletinus, Tylopilus, Gyrodon, Gyroporos, Fuscoboletinus, Boletellus,* etc. The differences among these segregate genera are so slight and, in general, so superficial, that the value of maintaining them is questionable and they will be ignored in this book.

Suillus and *Boletus* differ from each other in a number of ways, none of which is completely consistent: (1) the pores are generally much larger in *Suillus* than in *Boletus:* (2) the pore walls are thin and membranous in *Suillus,* thick and fleshy in *Boletus;* (3) the pore openings are often angular and uneven in *Suillus,* with one side of the pore wall often extending downward like a tooth, while they are generally round and uniform in *Boletus;* (4) the stems of *Suillus* are often glandular dotted while the stems of *Boletus* are often covered with a fine net or reticulum; (5) *Suillus* tends to have darker colored spores than *Boletus*—pale cinnamon to dark yellow-brown as opposed to dull yellow-brown to olive; (6) the spores of *Suillus* are often ornamented while those of *Boletus* are generally smooth; and (7) *Boletus* is primarily a European and eastern North American genus with very few species restricted to the West, while *Suillus* is a western North American genus with many species found only there.

While no species of *Suillus* are known to be poisonous, there are many species that have never been tested. In the East, any *Suillus* can probably be safely eaten, but in the West, where most of the untested species occur, caution is advised in eating members of this genus. I have taste tested some of the formerly untested western species and found some of them to be edible and good. Taste testing, however, is something to be undertaken only with great care and the use of caution. Most species of *Boletus* have been tested many times and, while most are edible, there are some very poisonous species in this genus.

All poisonous species of *Boletus* have either red pore

openings or flesh that turns blue when broken. Before eating any bolete, therefore, break open the cap and wait for at least one minute to see if the flesh gradually changes color. If it changes to blue, either do not eat it or else take special care in keying it to be sure it is an edible species. If the flesh of a *Boletus* species remains white, it will not be poisonous.

Boletus edulis is the choicest of all boletes. It is easily recognized by the following characteristics: (1) massive foot (base of stem) which is globe-shaped in young specimens, elongating into a club-shaped stem which may be 20 cm. long but is more commonly 8 to 15 cm.; (2) a faint net-like pattern on the upper stem; (3) cap some shade of tan or brown and hemispherical in shape, 10 to 20 cm. in diameter when mature (the record is over 30 cm. in diameter!); (4) pores with white openings when young which gradually change, first to yellow and then to yellowish green as the cap matures; (5) pore layer free from the stem; (6) flesh white and remains white when broken or bruised; and (7) olive brown spore sprint. There are two species which can easily be confused with *Boletus edulis,* but neither is poisonous. *B. olivaceobrunneus,* also known as *Tylopilus olivaceobrunneus,* has darker colored spores and a very pronounced net on the upper stem; it is often considered to be merely a variety or ecotype of *B. edulis* and is reported to be its equal as far as flavor is concerned. *B. felleus* also has a coarser net than *B. edulis,* has red or cinnamon-colored spores, and the flesh turns reddish when broken. In old specimens, the pore openings are reddish. The surest way to distinguish the two, however, is by tasting the flesh: *B. felleus* has a very bitter flavor which makes it unfit for human consumption, even though it is not poisonous, while the flavor of *B. edulis* resembles that of hazel nuts. *B edulis* is illustrated in Fig. 20.

Boletus edulis is often infested with worms, actually the maggots of a small fly. In young specimens, if there is no evidence of worms, the entire sporocarp, both cap and

Fig. 20. *Boletus edulis*, the king's bolete or cep.

stem, may be eaten. In older specimens, the pore layer is usually removed, since it is most likely to be infested, and the upper layer of the cap carefully examined for tell-tale pin holes.

Boletus aurantiacus is often more common than *B. edulis* and is considered by many mycophagists to be equally delicious. It has a large, orange or red cap, almost hemispherical in shape, with pale yellow pores when young which gradually become olive and then grayish brown as the sporocarps mature. It grows under pine or in spruce-fir forests and is common from late summer until late fall. When the fleshy part of the cap is broken, the white flesh gradually changes to a lilac-gray.

Common names for these two choice mushrooms are king bolete, or cep, and orange-cap bolete.

The rough-stemmed bolete, *B. scaber*, is similar in appearance to the orange-cap bolete but is usually smaller and more slender and the cap is grayish brown. It is edible but not as choice as the king bolete or the orange-cap; at times it is very abundant under birch or other deciduous trees.

In the fall of the year, species of *Suillus* become especially abundant; many of these, especially *S. borealis*, *S. lakei*, and *S. luteus*, are edible and choice. *S. subolivaceous* is common on eroded banks in forested areas of Idaho, under white pine in northern Idaho and under lodgepole and ponderosa pines in the Stanley Basin of central Idaho. The stalk is conspicuously glandular-dotted above and below the ring, which is very broad and slimy on the outer layer. The cap is typically 5 to 6 cm. in diameter and olive-brown; the stem is commonly about 2 cm. thick (Fig. 21). This species is listed in most mushroom books as untested; however, it has been taste tested by several people at Ricks College and rated good to choice.

Suillus borealis resembles *S. subolivaceous* in many ways, but lacks the glandular dots on the stem and has no annulus. The partial veil is lilac brown to chocolate and leaves colored patches on the underside of the cap along the margin. The stem is usually wine colored at the base, almost white above. Like many species of *Suillus,* the cap is slimy when wet, unpleasant to handle though a choice one to eat. It often grows on hard packed soil in white pine forests; the stem is so short that the caps appear to be resting on the ground (Fig. 22). Similar, but with a longer stem and darker spores is *Suillus spectabilis,* a rare species found in bogs under larch (photo on cover).

Several species of *Suillus* having slimy caps, especially *S. luteus,* are commonly called slippery jacks. The caps of *S. luteus* are very slimy and are dull dark reddish brown with yellow tubes. The ring is purplish to purplish brown and the stem above the ring is distinctly glandular-dotted. This species is often extremely abundant in jack pine woods and is gathered in large quantities. The slime is wiped from the cap with a paper towel or cloth and the tube layer is removed before eating; it is rated as one of the choicest of all mushrooms.

Two relatively uncommon boletes, *Boletus eastwoodiae,* commonly called Miss Alice East-

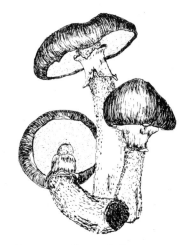

Fig. 21. *Suillus subolivaceous.*

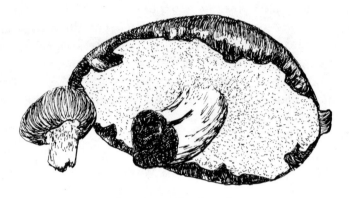

Fig. 22. *Suillus borealis.*

wood's bolete, and *B. satanus,* are very poisonous and must be carefully avoided. Eating either of them will lead to severe stomach cramps and digestive disturbances which may require hospitalization. When weather and soil conditions are right, either of them may be abundant, and they should be regarded as potential killers. They are both easily recognized, being characterized by red or scarlet pore openings and flesh which turns blue within about a minute after breaking open the cap. The stem is much more slender than that of the king bolete but is covered with the same type of fine net. Avoid all boletes that have red pore openings ! It is also wise to avoid boletes in which the flesh turns blue when broken, even though there are some good mushrooms, like *B. coerulescens,* in this category.

the eccentric white gilled mushrooms. Several species of lignicolous mushrooms (mushrooms which grow on logs and stumps) are rather common, and have a good to choice flavor. They are easily recognized by their white spores, gills, and caps attached at the margin to a substrate without stems, or caps attached slightly to distinctly off center with stems, and usually with decurrent gills.

Lentinus lepideus is an easily identified, relatively common mushroom which is highly variable in its general appearance as well as flavor. It can be recognized by its scaly cap, usually off center attachment to the stem, and serrate to crenulate gills. The caps are typically 10 to 15 cm. in diameter, but are frequently over 20 cm. in diameter in eastern Idaho, where most mushroom collectors rate it good to choice. In some places, it is typically too tough and strong in flavor to rate that high. The caps are rather dry and persist for several days or even weeks; consequently, it is sometimes the only edible mushroom that can be found during periods of prolonged drought in the West. It grows wherever conifers abound and frequently can be found on railroad ties, bridge railings, and similar locations. It is best cooked slowly with onions in butter, and one cap will often feed several people. It is frequently cut into flakes, dried, and stored, then used to flavor gravies and sauces. The serrate gills are so distinctive that there is no danger of confusing this mushroom with any poisonous species. It is therefore an excellent choice for the beginning mycophagist to learn (Fig. 23).

The genus *Pleurotus* is easily recognized by the white gills and spore print, stem attached to the margin of the cap, and many sporocarps in a clump forming overlapping layers (Fig. 24). Two species are especially delicious. The oyster mushroom *P. ostreatus,* grows in large clumps on cottonwood, maple, or other hardwood logs; the caps are shell-like, giving it the appearance of oysters. The angel wing mushroom, *P. porrigens,* has broader and lighter colored caps than the oyster mushroom and is common on conifers.

Fig. 23. *Lentinus lepideus.* Note the serrate gill edges which distinguish this species from almost all other mushrooms.

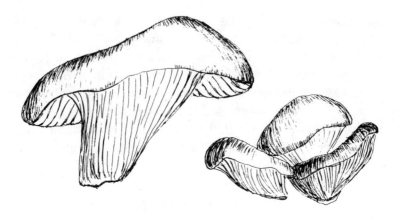

Fig. 24. *Pleurotus ostreatus,* The oyster mushroom. The common name refers to the shell-like sporocarps which have a delicate, pearl-like color, rather than to the flavor. They are often prepared for eating in the same way oysters are prepared.

Both the oyster mushroom and angel's wings have a pleasantly mild flavor. The oyster mushroom is a long-lived perennial, and once you have found a fruiting log, you will keep coming back to it year after year. Some people take the logs home and water them, whereupon the sporocarps keep coming out for a long period of time.

Pleurotus serotinus resembles the oyster mushroom but fruits later and has a bluish gray cap as opposed to pearly gray, and yellow instead of white gills. It is edible, but of poor quality, being rather bitter.

With their white spores, white decurrent gills, and eccentric attachment of cap to stem, the oyster mushroom and angel's wings are seldom confused with other mushrooms, either edible or poisonous. For example *Crepidotus* and other Cortinariaceae have brown spores. *Lentinus* is readily distinguished by its wavy gill edges, almost centrally attached cap, and only slightly decurrent gills. The caps of *Panus* are covered with a dense reddish fuzz and the gills are pale tan. *Lenzites* has stemless caps that are beautifully zoned in orange, gray, and tan.

the common dark gilled mushrooms. There are several species of mushrooms having dark gills, purplish or chocolate brown to black spores, and free or adnexed to adnate gills that are good to eat. There are also several species of poisonous mushrooms having this combination of characteriestics that one needs to guard against.

The genera *Agaricus* and *Coprinus* are of special value; in addition, many mushroom hunters like the flavor of some of the species of *Stropharia*. These three genera are relatively safe providing certain precautions are taken: (1) Be sure the spore print is purplish to black, not brown. Poisonous members of the brown-spored Cortinariaceae, such as *Hebeloma crustuliniforme, Inocybe pudica,* or even *Galerina venenata,* could be confused with *Agaricus* and *Stropharia* unless spore print color is carefully observed. (2) Guard against poisonous species of *Panaeolus* which are easily confused with *Coprinus* since both genera have black spores; *Coprinus insignus* is also reported to be poisonous. (3) Watch out for *Naematoloma fasciculare, Agaricus hondensis,* and *A. subrutiliescens* which are poisonous and, like edible species of *Agaricus* and *Stropharia,* have purplish to chocolate brown spores. (4) Check for changes in flesh color. The *Psilocybe* species are difficult to distinguish from *Stropharia* (and could be confused with *Agaricus)*; however, the flesh of either the cap or the base of the stem of the poisonous psilocybes stain blue or green when bruised.

Some species of *Agaricus* are especially choice; the common meadow champignon, *Agaricus campestris,* is regarded by many people to be the equal of the morels and the king bolete. Several varieties of *A. campestris*—variously known as *A. brunnescens, A. bisporus, Psalliota campestris,* or *P. bisporus*—are cultivated commercially; this is the common store mushroom.

The genus *Agaricus* is recognized by its free gills, purplish-brown spore print, tapered base (or at least not swollen at the base), and ring but no volva. The gills are pink in young specimens but turn purplish to chocolate brown as the spores mature. The genus contains species which are poisonous to some people. Fortunately, the poisonous species are easy to recognize having one or more of the following characteristics: (1) a creosote-like odor, (2) vinaceous brown fibrils on the upper surface of the cap and especially near the margins, and/or (3) an intense yellow stain that develops wherever the flesh is bruised (even by touching in many cases).

Three genera that are frequently confused with *Agaricus* are *Stropharia, Naematoloma,* and *Pholiota.* According to several authorities, none of the *Stropharias* or *Pholiotas* are poisonous with the exception of a European species, *S. depilata;* however, some people have reported mild disturbances following eating *S. aeruginosa, S. squamosa, P. hiemalis,* or *P. squarrosa.* On the other hand, *Naematoloma fasciculare* is definitely poisonous, but is so bitter that it is seldom eaten in quantities great enough to cause any problems. Another non-poisonous species, *S. ambigua,* smells and tastes like rotting leaves. *Pholiota* has brown spores, not purplish as in *Agaricus, Stropharia,* and *Naematoloma,* and can, therefore, be recognized when a good spore print is taken. *Stropharia,* and *Naematoloma* have adnexed to sinuate gills, not the completely free gills that *Agaricus* has; but remember that it is difficult to distinguish between free gills and adnexed gills unless one examines the apex of the stem very closely.

Agaricus campestris is a common lawn and pasture mushroom, one of several which form "fairy rings." After a rain in late summer or fall, it is frequently very abundant and will usually be found in the same lawn or grassy opening in the woods several years in a row. Other edible species include *A. silvicola, A. nivescens,* and "the prince," *A. augustus.* Other edible mushrooms which resemble *A. campestris* and its relatives are *Stropharia coronilla, S. rugosaannulata, Naematoloma capnoides, Pholiota aurea, P. caperata, P. squarrosoides,* and *P. terrestris.* Although I rate it very mediocre, hardly worth trying, some of my students have rated *Stropharia coronilla* one of the best tasting of all the mushrooms we try.

Most gourmets prefer to eat *Agaricus campestris*, the common meadow champignon, in the button stage. There have been some deaths as a result of this because *A. campestris* and *Amanita muscaria* have very similar ecological characteristics, often grow together, and are difficult to tell apart at the button stage. The base of the *Agaricus* stem is tapered whereas that of the *Amanita* stem is swollen. When collecting *A. campestris* in the button stage, every button must be carefully and individually examined. It is much safer to eat only store buttons. Many mycophagists eat wild champignons only after the caps have matured to the stage where the gills have turned purplish, or chocolate brown in the case of *A. nivescens.*

Some mushroom hunters prefer the *Coprinus* or inky caps over most other mushrooms. When fully mature, inky caps are easily identified because the gills have dissolved into a black, inky fluid. At this stage, the sporocarps are not fit to eat, however. In a given clump of *Coprinus*, some sporocarps will be older than others, and the young specimens are not only edible but have a nice flavor. Deliquescing begins at the margin of the cap and proceeds inward until finally even the top of the stem has been dissolved. When deliquescence has just begun, the margins may be removed and the rest of the cap eaten. *Coprinus* specimens must be eaten very soon after collecting before the process of autodigestion turns the gills into liquid. The shaggy mane, *C. comatus*, can be kept for two or three days by storing in cold water; probably other *Coprinus* species can be stored in the same way.

Coprinus atramentarius and *C. micaceus* are both edible and good, though not as choice as *C. comatus*. Both grow in clumps, often coming up in lawns near stumps of elm or other hardwoods following summer rains. As the name suggests, *Coprinus* species are often coprophilous; however it is recommended that specimens growing on manure be avoided because of the danger of confusion with species of *Panaeolus.* The caps of both species are broadly parabolic. When young, the sporocarps of *Coprinus* have white or gray gills; as they mature the gills gradually turn black and finally deliquesce.

A European species, *Coprinus insignis,* is poisonous, and several species of *Coprinus* are too small to be of any value as table mushrooms. All other species in this genus are edible although *C. atramentarius* contains appreciable quantities of a disulfiram-like toxin which reacts with alcohol and should never be consumed within 48 hours before or after drinking an alcoholic beverage.

The genus *Panaeolus,* which is similar in appearance to the inky caps, contains several very poisonous species. Gills of young *Coprinus* sporocarps are white to gray and gradually turn black as they mature; young sporocarps of *Panaeolus* have mottled gills that never deliquesce with age. *P. separatus* and *P. campanulatus* are both definitely poisonous, causing hallucinations; it is possible that if eaten in large quantity they could prove fatal. The haymaker's mushroom, *P. foenicesii,* is commonly eaten but there are reports of illness after doing so that have cast suspicion on it. *Panaeolus* species are very common in the West, occurring in grassland on cow and horse dung. Before eating any mushroom in this group—*Agaricus, Stropharia,* or *Coprinus*—check the keys in Chapter Five carefully to be 100% certain of your identification.

russulas and milky caps. The Russulaceae have white spores and thick, brittle stems that often snap like a piece of chalk, even when fresh. When young, species of *Lactarius* exude a milky latex when the stems or caps are broken; the other genus, *Russula,* lacks the milky latex. The characteristics of each genus are so distinctive that there is no danger of confusing either of them with any other genus of mushrooms. There are both edible and poisonous species in each genus.

In the West, *Russula* species are common, but milky caps are rare. One of the common late summer species which has a mild but pleasant flavor is *Russula brevipes*. It has a very short stem with decurrent gills extending over halfway to the base (Fig. 25A). The spore print is white or very pale cream colored. The cap is a dingy brown, deeply depressed in the center, dry and usually covered with bits of duff adhering as it pushes through the soil, and has a rounded margin. The stem is white to dingy brown; the gills are white or slightly off-white. *R. brevipes* grows on forest litter in coniferous forests, fruiting in late summer after heavy rains or in the fall.

Russula brevipes is listed in many books as *R. delica*, a European species. Actually, it is very similar in appearance to both *R. delica* and *R. cascadensis*, differing from the former only by spore charactistics and its narrow gills that are closely spaced, and from the latter by flesh color. *R. cascadensis* has white flesh like *R. brevipes*, but the flesh

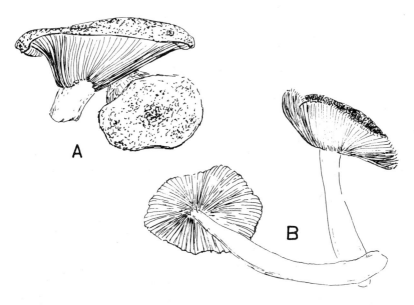

Fig. 25. Two common species of *Russula:* **A.** *Russula brevipes,* **B.** *Russula emetica.*

turns pale brownish where bruised; it also has a peppery flavor when tasted raw. All three are edible.

Several species of *Russula* have red to purple convex caps and adnate gills. The largest of these is *R. alutacea* with caps 8 to 20 cm. in diameter or sometimes larger. Its cap is dull red or red-violet and it has a mild and pleasant flavor like *R. brevipes.* The stem is white, tinged with red, and the gills are pale yellow, becoming brownish with age. It is an excellent mushroom and dries well for winter storage and use. Similar to it is another good mushroom, *R. xerampelina,* which is purple, varying somewhat in color, and has the odor of shrimps when old or dry or while cooking. The white gills bruise yellowish.

Resembling in appearance both of the above is another red species, *Russula emetica,* which is poisonous (Fig. 25 B). The color is brighter than that of *R. alutacea* and the caps are generally smaller, but is most easily distinguished by its peppery flavor. Always taste test red capped russulas and never eat any with a strong, peppery flavor. *R. rosacea* is another red capped *Russula* with peppery flavor that is **suspected** of being poisonous though some reports indicate it is harmless. It is strongly recommended that you avoid it, beyond the small bit that you taste test for identification.

Two other edible species found in the West are *Russula aeruginea,* which has flat, or sometimes slightly depressed, dull green caps that are somewhat slimy when wet, and *R. olivacea* with more rounded, very large caps, that are olive or olive mixed with red. Both grow in conifer forests. Mild flavored *R. aeruginea* has almost white gills that spot brown where injured, the spore print is pale yellow, and the base of the stem has cinnamon buff discolorations. *R. olivacea* caps are commonly 10 to 15 cm. in diameter but are sometimes as much as 35 cm. The sporocarps are edible but of rather poor quality.

Because of their stout, fleshy-fibrous to brittle stems, and robust appearance, milky caps are easily confused with russulas. Examine carefully all specimens that resemble a russula for the presence of a latex or milky juice. Do not eat any that have a watery latex or a latex that is milky white or violet-tinged. Milky caps with blood red latex or more or less orange colored latex are generally safe.

Lactarius sanguifluus is the best of the milky caps. It is recognized by the blood red latex which can be observed by cutting the apex of the stem with a sharp razor. It is most abundant west of the Cascades and is found in late summer or fall under pine or douglas fir. More common is L. deliciosus which has a somewhat orange latex when first exposed but gradually changes to a greenish color. It is common in wet conifer forests in summer and fall, often under Devil's Club. Different collections vary considerably in flavor, some being choice, others of poor quality. The sporocarps are commonly 15 cm. in diameter and often wormy. Bruised areas in both species tend to stain green.

Four species of Lactarius are poisonous or suspected of being poisonous and should be avoided. The most dangerous of these is Lactarius aspideus. It has yellow caps and gills, the gills staining violaceous where injured or bruised, and violet or white changing to violet latex. L. scrobiculatus, L. torminosus, and L. aquifluus are among the species having white or watery latex which are also poisonous.

additional edible mushrooms. There are literally
hundreds of species of mushrooms that are known to be edible. Some of these are choice while others are very mediocre; some are easily recognized while others can be identified only with great effort. Danger of confusion with a poisonous species is slight to non-existent in some species, while with others even the experts have a difficult time being sure. We cannot list here the distinguishing characteristics of all of these edible species, but we can point out some groups that are worth knowing better. Chief among these are the chanterelles, because some of them are

especially choice; and the tooth mushrooms and coral fungi, because identification of the good mushrooms having interesting flavors is so easy in these groups.

The chanterelles have blunt veins, rather than gills, and usually a trumpet shaped cap. There are many mushrooms with trumpet caps and decurrent gills, however, that amateur mushroom hunters often confuse with chanterelles. Pictures, even colored photographs, are not always much help. If the thickness of the "gills" is almost as great as the width, and if smaller crossveins can be seen between the veins, the mushroom is a chanterelle. If the gills are much wider than they are thick and if the gills are almost knife edge sharp, the mushroom is not a chanterelle even though the cap may resemble a funnel with definitely decurrent gills.

Cantharellus cibarius (Fig. 26) is one of the choicest of all mushrooms. The cap is golden, often the color of an egg yolk, smooth, shaded with tan and slightly convex when if first breaks through the soil but becoming funnel shaped with a distinctive wavy margin later on. A typical specimen is 10 cm. tall and 15 cm. in diameter. The main veins are narrow, sometimes gill-like, and the crossveins are prominent. The base of the stem is often slightly swollen. It is found in the fall in old hemlock, spruce, or douglas fir forests.

Cantharellus subalbidus is also choice. The veins are very narrow and close together resembling gills, but the crossveins, though sparse, give it away as a chanterelle. It is white or slightly dingy and short and stocky with veins extending to the base of the stem. Where injured, the flesh stains rusty yellow to orange, finally changing to orange-brown.

At least two species of chanterelles are poisonous, at least to some people. *Cantharellus floccosus* has a narrow trumpet-shaped sporocarp which is hollow from early stages on to maturity, and with the hollow, at first, lined with delicate scales. *C. kauffmanii* flares out more than

Fig. 26. *Cantharellus cibarius,* the common chanterelle.

C. floccosus but not as much as *C. cibarius* and *C. subalbidus* and has dull brown strap-like scales lining the bottom of the funnel. The veins in both of these species are more "chanterelle-like" than in the previous two and sometimes form shallow pores. Both are found in conifer forests as are the other chanterelles described here.

Closely related to the chanterelles are the coral mushrooms, Clavariaceae. They are recognized by their upright, usually branching habit, giving them the appearance of coral. Only one species of coral fungus is known to be poisonous and it is easy to identify. Several species are bitter, tough, or otherwise inedible, but there are also some very good mushrooms in this group.

Ramaria gelatinosa is the poisonous species. It is easily recognized by the gelatinous, almost transparent tissue in the center of the sporocarp near its base and white flesh which turns red-brown to black when bruised. Avoid all coral fungi in which the flesh near the base of the plant is rubbery and translucent like cold gelatin. *Ramaria formosa* is also listed in many books as poisonous; however, it is very difficult to distinguish between these two species, and the poisonings blamed on *R. formosa* may be cases of mistaken identity. Nevertheless, use caution in eating *R. formosa*: Be sure that it really is *R. formosa* and then, taste test a small piece before preparing your specimens for a meal.

The cauliflower mushroom, *Sparassis radicata* (Fig. 35), is one of the choicest of the coral group. The large clusters, typically 25 cm. in diameter, resemble large heads of lettuce or clusters of egg noodles because the branches are flattened. It fruits in the fall in old-growth conifer forests. *Ramaria pyxidata* and *R. botrytis* are also good species that are easily recognized by their multiple branches and mild, pleasant flavor. The former fruits in the spring and early summer on dead wood, usually poplar or willow, and the latter is found under both hardwoods and conifers in the fall.

Also closely related to the chanterelles are the tooth mushrooms, the Hydnaceae. Most of the species in this family look like gill mushrooms until the bottom side is examined; then the distinctive teeth are seen. Two species grow on trees and resemble polypores very closely. None of the species are known to be poisonous although some of the bitter ones may be—these are so bitter that it is inconceivable that anyone would try to eat them. On the other hand, some of the choicest of all mushrooms are found in this family.

Of the more than 100 species of Hydnaceae found in North America, *Hydnum repandum*, the hedgehog fungus, also known as *Dentinum repandum*, is one of the choicest and vies with any mushroom for delicious flavor. It can be used in almost any dish calling for mushrooms but is often prepared with cauliflower, zucchini, green onions, celery, carrots, and green pepper and sautéed in butter. This is a late summer to late fall mushroom often found in mixed forests but also in coniferous forests. The cap is dry, buff to

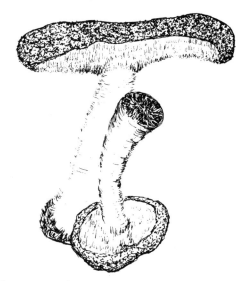

Fig. 27. *Hydnum repandum,* also known as *Dentinum repandum.*

Fig. 28. *Hericium coralloides,* the coral tooth fungus, similar to the bear's head fungus, *H. caput-ursi.*

orange or faded orange, with thick, soft, brittle, light yellow flesh and cream colored teeth that are about 4 to 8 mm. long; the cap is broadly convex with a wavy margin (Fig. 27), 1.5 to 10 cm. broad.

Another good mushroom is *Hericium coralloides* (Fig. 28), the bear's head fungus or coral hydnum. It consists of a large tuber-like mass of tissue, branched like a coral fungus, with long teeth (10 to 25 mm. long) hanging down from the branches. The sporocarps are usually pure white, but may be yellowish in age. It is attached to logs of hardwoods and conifers fruiting in late summer and fall. Since all of the *Hericium* species are edible, no great harm has been done if you misidentify this one. Other species include *H. ramosum*, *H. weirii*, and *H. erinaceous*. *H. coralloides* is also known as *H. caput-ursi*.

The fried chicken mushroom, *Lyophyllum multiceps*, also known as *Clitocybe multiceps*, is a gill mushroom with white spore print considered especially choice by many mycophagists, though others classify it as mediocre. All agree that it has a very different flavor from all other mushrooms. It is easily recognized providing some precautions are taken including a good spore print. It occurs in thick grass or leaves on clay soil following heavy rains in late summer or fall, occasionally in early spring, and it grows in large clumps of typically 20 or 30 sporocarps joined at the base. The stems are flattened and/or curved, because of the growth form, and are attached centrally on the caps with gills slightly decurrent to adnate. The gills are white, as are the spores; the caps are creamy to tan and feel soapy, when moistened, smooth, persistently rounded, and up to 10 to 15 cm. in diameter. The flesh is white and firm.

The species most likely to be confused with *L. multiceps* is the **deadly poisonous** *Entoloma sinuatum*. Both have a pleasant odor when fresh and both grow in clumps often hidden in tall grass. Their similarities and differences were discussed in Chapter Three. Before eating a mushroom that you think is the fried chicken mushroom, check carefully the following characteristics: (1) be sure your specimens are growing in clusters of at least five or more and discard **all** solitary specimens even though you are certain they are the same species; (2) note the soapy feeling of the moistened cap; and (3) examine the spore print carefully so that you are positive it is white and not pale pink. When you take the spore print, place a cover slip under part of the cap and examine the spores under a microscope; if they are angular or almost round but slightly angular, discard your collection—or donate it to a herbarium—even though the spore print was white. The spores of *Lyophyllum* fall slowly; be sure to put a damp piece of tissue paper or cotton on the cap under the tumbler as you prepare your spore print.

additional poisonous mushrooms. Although the

most deadly poisonous mushrooms were described in Chapter Three, there are other species that can cause considerable discomfort. Smith, in his "Field Guide to Western Mushrooms," listed *Gyromitra infula, Boletus satanus, Tricholoma pardinum, Chlorophyllum molybdites, Inocybe pudica, Clitocybe illudens, Coprinus insignis,* and *Lactarius aspideus,* in addition to the Fatal Five, as especially dangerous. All are widespread in the East, the West, and Europe. No one should taste test or experiment with any mushroom that resembles or may be closely related to these dangerous species. It has been said that there are two kinds of mycophagists: Old ones and bold ones—but few who are both. See Chapter Six for descriptions of these genera.

There are at least three or four dozen additional species of mushrooms in North America that are known to be slightly to moderately poisonous. Unless eaten in large quantity, they seldom pose a threat to health or life, but they can cause discomfort. Among the hundreds of untested species, there may be some as poisonous as the

Fatal Five; if so, they probably belong to one or another of four or five families, especially the Amanitaceae, Tricholomataceae, Entolomataceae, or Cortinariaceae. Species of Amanitaceae and Entolomataceae known to be deadly poisonous were discussed in Chapter Three.

Several genera of the Cortinariaceae contain poisonous mushrooms; three genera, *Galerina, Inocybe,* and *Hebeloma* possibly contain only poisonous species. Poisonous, as well as edible, species are also known in the genus *Cortinarius,* whereas most, if not all, species of *Pholiota* and *Rozites* are non-poisonous, often edible and good. The toxin found in *Galerina,* amanitin, was discussed in Chapter Three; it is "type 1," a protoplasmic poison. *Inocybe* toxins are "type 3," similar to the muscarine type which occurs in *Amanita muscaria* and sometimes causes death. Muscarine cannot be removed by parboiling, so the only recommendation we can make for *Inocybe* is that it be avoided! The exact type of toxin in the *Hebeloma* species is unknown except that it causes gastric disturbances (type 2). *Hebeloma crustuliniforme* is commonly called "poison pie," and it is suspected of having caused deaths.

There are hundreds of species of Cortinariaceae that are extremely difficult even for the experts to identify. They are small, have caps, gills, and stems varying from pale tan to dark brown, and are found everywhere. Most mushroom collectors call them LBM's (little brown mushrooms) and then ignore them, leaving their identification to mycological specialists who study their spores and biochemical characteristics in detail. Most LBM's have brown spores, but some have black or pale colored spores; LBM's belong, therefore, to several families, and many genera, of mushrooms. In any genus in which LBM's occur, there are often other species which are large and easily identified. Probably most LBM's are members of the Cortinariaceae with *Galerina* and *Inocybe* being among the genera containing some of them.

The Tricholomataceae is another family known to include several poisonous species. The family contains several good to choice mushrooms: e.g. *Armillaria mellea, Pleurotus ostreatus, Marasmius oreades, Lyophyllum multiceps,* and *Lentinus lepideus.* It also contains several species of poisonous mushrooms. The most dangerous of these are *Clitocybe dealbata* and *Tricholoma pardinum,* but *C. illudens* and *C. aurantiaca* are also reported to be poisonous. *Colybia dryophila* is frequently eaten but some people have reported gastro-intestinal disturbances after eating it. *Clitocybe dealbata* has a dull white cap, convex to flat and then depressed in age, with white stem, gills, and spore print. The gills are narrow, close, and extend down the stem. It grows in lawns with *Agaricus campestris* and *Stropharia coronilla* but is much smaller than them, and one might carelessly includes a specimen or two of this species in a batch of champignons thinking they were young specimens. *Tricholoma pardinum* is a much larger mushroom with adnexed gills and a low, broad knob on an almost flat, white cap. The gills and spore print are also white. It is common in the fall under conifers.

The family of mushrooms responsible for a vast majority of deaths from fungus poisons is, of course, the Amanitaceae. A morphologically similar family, the Lepiotaceae, contains poisonous species, the most dangerous being *Chlorophyllum molybdites.* Like the *Amanitas, Chlorophyllum* has free gills, a prominent ring, and a bulbous stem; however, it has no volva and the spore print is green. Closely related is *Lepiota naucina,* an edible species which causes gastric disturbances in some people, and is so easily confused with *Amanita phalloides* and *A. virosa* that I strongly recommend against eating it.

While there is no single rule that will distinguish between edible and poisonous mushrooms, there are some guidelines that can assist in recognizing and avoiding poisonous species. Take special care in identifying, or else avoid, mushrooms in the following categories: (1) Ascomycetes in which the cap is smooth or wrinkled rather than pitted; (2) fleshy pore mushrooms in which the flesh turns blue where broken and exposed to air and/or have red pore openings; (3) gill mushrooms having white spores, free gills, and bulbous stem base; (4) little brown mushrooms with or without reddish tints, having brown spores; (6) gill mushrooms which exude white, clear, or lilac colored latex when the stem or cap is cut or broken; and (7) mushrooms with black gills, that may be mottled, which do not deliquesce with age, and/or which grow on cow or horse manure.

Many poisonous mushrooms are poisonous only to some people, often to people who are convalescing from some illness; many are only slightly poisonous; some cause slight to severe hallucinations or slight nervousness; a few have poisons that can be removed by parboiling. Hallucinogenic mushrooms occur in *Inocybe, Psilocybe, Amanita,* and *Panaeolus. Panaeolus campanulatus* and *P. retirugis* are both known as Divine Mushrooms, referring to their hallucinogenic properties. The latter is used in Mexico in certain religious rites. Several species of mushroom— including *Gyromitra* and *Helvella* species, *Amanita muscaria, Lactarius rufus,* and *L. torminosus*—contain toxins which can be removed by parboiling; however, only *Lactarius torminosus* and some of the false morels *(Gyromitra* and *Helvella)* are very good. The other species are not worth the bother (and possible risk) of parboiling, though they are edible. Remember to throw away the water immediately after parboiling any mushroom!

The Russians look at parboiling from a different point of view. *Amanita muscaria* was once regarded as a sort of poor man's substitute for alcohol. The Russian peasants understood the secret of parboiling, but they kept the water and threw away the mushroom. The hallucinogenic drugs in *A. muscaria* are apparently addictive, for there are reports that during drought years, when mushrooms are hard to obtain, single caps of *A. muscaria* sold for as much as 20 rubles, a ruble being worth slightly more than a dollar. This hardly sounds like a poor man's substitute for alcohol!

The most frequently asked question of every mushroom hunter is this: "Is this a mushroom or a toadstool?" But what is a toadstool? Perhaps you have seen pictures in Scandinavian story books of big fat toads sitting comfortably on *Amanita muscaria,* the "common toadstool." If so, you likely drew the logical conclusion that the word "toadstool" was of Scandinavian origin referring to some saga having to do with toads. Since Scandinavians are great lovers of nature, what could be more logical? You are half right. The word is of Scandinavian origin, but it comes from the words *döds stol* (pronounced doods stool) which means "the chair of death." From early times the term "toadstool" has been reserved for those species of mushrooms which are poisonous, and especially *Amanita muscaria,* the colorful, common toadstool which is responsible for the majority of mushroom poisonings that occur each year and for a fair share of deaths.

taste testing mushrooms. There are only two sure ways of finding out whether a mushroom is poisonous or edible: (1) follow up on medical cases of poisoning, and (2) taste testing. The former is not always reliable; if the victim had known what the mushroom was before he ate it, he probably would never have eaten it, and therefore he probably won't be able to identify the same species with absolute certainty after (or if) he recovers. Furthermore, many mushroom eaters mix their species so it may be impossible to tell which one poisoned the victim. In taste testing, the mycophagist makes certain of the identification of his species first and then eats a small part of it and watches carefully for symptoms of stomach or nerve disorders, including drowsiness. Perhaps the champion of all taste testers is Bengt Cortin, author of one of the best mushroom handbooks for northern Europe. Several years

ago, Cortin had taste tested 354 species, many of them for confirmation of previous records, including over 40 completely new species in such taxonomic groups as the very risky genus *Cortinarius*. There are rules, however, that must be stringently followed if one is to be a successful taste tester.

The reason I present these rules here is that I am acutely aware of how frequently amateurs make mistakes in keying unknown species of plants. I urge my students, therefore, to taste test every edible mushroom that they key out but have not tried before, as though it were a new species. If a new specimen they are trying keys to a good or choice species that they are anxious to taste and enjoy, I urge them to follow the taste testing rules carefully and patiently before they prepare a meal. I do not encourage them to taste test species that are listed as "edibility unknown" in the mushroom books. This can be left to professionals, like Bengt Cortin, who have available the latest chemical methods for detecting known toxins, as well as much more knowledge.

The first rule for taste testing is (1) **know** the *Amanitas* ! and **never** taste test any *Amanita* ! Some botanists have split the genus into several genera—*Amanitopsis, Amidella, Aspidella,* and *Vaginata,* for example—but if you know the characteristics of the *Amanitas,* you won't need tc worry about the new names. Closely related genera, like *Limacella* and *Lepiota,* are best avoided, too. Likewise, know the remaining Fatal Five and never taste test any of them, especially the *Entolomas, Galerinas,* and their relatives.

The other rules for taste testing are (2) test only one species at a time; wait at least 24 to 48 hours before testing a second species; (3) taste the mushroom raw and note carefully any bitter, peppery, or unpleasant flavors; disqualify any species having such flavors; (4) watch carefully for any sulfur after-tastes or signs of digestive disturbance, and for any light headedness, dizzy feelings, or drowsiness; (5) wait at least half an hour after tasting the raw mushroom, fry a piece of the mushroom in a small amount of shortening and eat a very small portion; watch for signs of digestive disturbance or other symptoms for at least twelve hours; and (6) have others test the same mushroom with you so that you have an idea of how it affects more than one person.

A piece of mushroom the size of a pea is large enough for the raw test; if any unpleasant flavor is noted, the rest of the piece can be spit out. Chew this piece very carefully, rolling the flesh around the tongue and against the palate so that the taste buds have plenty of opportunity to come in contact with it. If the mushroom passes the raw test, take a slightly larger piece for the cooked test and repeat the procedure. If it passes both tests, you may have found a mushroom that you will want to prepare for yourself and your family in the future.

preparing mushrooms for the table. When a good "stand" of mushrooms has been found, the first step in preparing them for the table is to collect them individually, examining each one to be sure that it is free of worms or spoilage and that all are of the same species. You should have a good wicker basket or reasonable substitute, a shoe box, for example, with strings attached to the four corners to form a handle; and a supply of waxed paper. The sporocarps may be wrapped individually in wax paper or a few of the same species may be wrapped together. Never wrap mushrooms of different species together! Simply twist the end of the wrapping to hold the package together. Never wrap them in plastic! While I recommend a firm, rigid container for collecting mushrooms because there is less danger of breaking or bruising the sporocarps, I frequently collect in a large grocery bag, especially if I am after one kind of mushroom—morels, for example. But I never collect in plastic bags; the sporocarps "sweat" and soon become rather unpleasant to handle or eat.

Before cooking, the mushrooms must be cleaned. The

fast way is to dump them in a sink full of water as you might clean carrots or potatoes. The preferred way is to wipe each sporocarp individually with a damp cloth or paper towel. As you clean them, check for evidence of worms or spoilage. Remove any wormy specimens. If only the base of the stem is wormy, it may be cut away, then examine the sporocarp carefully for evidence of tell-tale pin holes, especially in the flesh just above the gill or pore layer. If there are pin holes in the cap, don't try to save the fruit—it will almost certainly be wormy.

After the sporocarps are cleaned and all spoiled, wormy, or over mature parts removed, they may be peeled, depending on the species, and cut into small pieces or sliced, and prepared for cooking. Dozens of recipes are available; some have already been presented in Chapter Two. A favorite, however, is a very simple one: Simply fry with onions in butter. This is a favorite over the campfire as well as in the kitchen, and any meat or vegetable dish tastes better when accompanied by wild mushrooms prepared this way. Because seasonings tend to impair the delicate mushroom flavor, *Farmers Bulletin 796,* "Some Common Edible and Poisonous Mushrooms," recommends cooking without any seasoning except butter, pepper, and salt. "Mushrooms may be prepared for the table in any way which would be suitable for oysters," says the *Bulletin.*

For the best results in preparing mushrooms, care must be taken not to overwhelm the flavor of the mushrooms with other ingredients. Some herbs enhance the mushroom flavor; others overpower it. Shallots, onions, chives, and garlic go well with mushrooms; many gourmets prefer shallots over the other members of the onion group. Butter and olive oil are superior to other shortenings. For raw mushroom spreads, whipping cream and cream cheeses are good. Parsley, pennyroyal, catnip, and oregano are favorite herbs to use in preparing mushroom dishes; cloves, pepper, and nutmeg are the spices gourmets prefer. Lemon juice, a small amount of tomato juice or diced green pepper, or dry wine may be added to many mushroom dishes. Mushrooms always improve the flavor of roasts or steaks: This is especially true with lamb, mutton, or game, the flavors of which seem to blend especially well with mushrooms. Eggplants, artichokes, green tomatoes, and green peppers are among the vegetables which are especially delicious when prepared with mushrooms.

A few recipes follow.

deviled mushrooms

1 qt. cultivated or wild mushrooms, seasoned with salt and
    pepper
1 pt. bread crumbs
4 eggs, 2 hard boiled, 2 raw
1/4 lb. butter
1 cup milk or cream (lemon juice may be substituted)

Mix the mashed yolks of the hard-boiled eggs with the raw eggs and stir into the milk or cream. Put a layer of crumbs in the bottom of a baking dish, then a layer of diced mushrooms, sprinkle over bits of butter and add part of the cream mixture; continue with alternating layers of crumbs and mushrooms until the dish is full, having bread crumbs and butter for the top layer. Bake for 20 minutes, closely covered, in a hot oven; then uncover for 5 minutes, or long enough for the top to be well browned.

mushrooms baked with tomatoes

In a baking dish, arrange small round slices of buttered toast, and upon each piece place a rather thin slice of tomato, salted and peppered. On each slice of tomato place a fine, thick mushroom, gill side up, and in the center of each put a generous piece of butter. Season with pepper and salt. Cover the dish and bake in a hot oven for 10 minutes; then uncover and bake for an additional 5 to 10 minutes, as needed.

stuffed peppers

1 pt. of mushrooms, cultivated or wild, seasoned with salt and pepper
6 peppers—stem ends, seeds, and white membrane removed
1 cup chopped chicken, veal, or game
½ lb. butter
1 tbs. water

Arrange the pepper on end in a baking dish with the water in the bottom of the dish. Cut the mushrooms into small pieces and mix with the meat; press this firmly into the peppers and top with a good-sized lump of butter. Melt the remaining butter and add to bottom of baking dish. Place the dish in a hot oven, cook covered for 15 minutes, then uncover and baste, and cook for 10 to 15 minutes longer, or until the peppers are perfectly tender.

clove-stuffed mushrooms

2 doz. medium to large mushrooms, cultivated or wild
1 cup shredded cheddar cheese
½ cup finely chopped onion
½ cup cooked, crumbled bacon
¼ tsp. ground cloves

Line mushrooms, stem side up, on a shallow, greased baking pan. Preheat oven to 450 F. Mix shredded cheddar cheese, onion, and bacon; stuff and pack mushrooms generously and sprinkle with a dash of cloves on top. Bake 5 to 10 minutes until bubbling. Serve warm.

cream of mushroom soup I

The best cream of mushroom soup is made from wild mushrooms, especially morels, but boletes and champignons are also good, as are others. The first recipe is from Margaret McKenny's chapter in "The Savory Wild Mushroom" by McKenny and Stuntz:

1 lb. chanterelles or other wild mushrooms
2 tbs. butter
2 cups milk
1 cup cream
1 tsp. minced parsley
flour, salt, pepper

Chop the mushrooms coarsely and roll in flour; sauté them gently in the butter until they are tender, but do not allow them to brown. Add the milk, cream, salt, and parsley. Heat almost to boiling and serve hot.

cream of mushroom soup II

From the chapter by Angelo M. Pellegrini in the book mentioned above.

wild mushrooms, preferably morels
shallots
parsley
butter
olive oil
chicken broth
pinch of nutmeg

Partially cook the mushrooms in butter and oil with the shallots and parsley. Cream them in a blender and finish cooking in just enough chicken broth to yield a dense but fluid soup. Add nutmeg and simmer for 15 minutes. Any soup not used may be put in quart containers and frozen. You will have to use your own judgment as to the exact balance of ingredients to use; be careful not to overwhelm the mushroom flavor with butter, broth, or herbs.

Any mushrooms not eaten fresh may be frozen or dried and saved for winter use. Frozen mushrooms are best prepared by cooking them with the same seasoning you use for the table and then freeze them in well sealed containers. They will keep for over a year without noticable deterioration. They can also be prepared by sautéing them, seasoned according to taste, and then reducing them to a paste in a blender. The paste is then frozen in small containers and used to enrich gravy or other sauces.

Any mushroom may be dried, but some dry much easier than others. One of the more difficult species, but undoubtedly the choicest, is *Boletus edulis.* Drying seems actually to strengthen and enhance its flavor and aroma, just the opposite of other mushrooms. Chefs at fancy restaurants prefer dried king bolete over all other mushrooms in making their special sauces. The commercial product is imported from the Balkans and at 1980 prices cost about $80 per pound in East Coast cities.

To dry mushrooms, first trim them and clean with a soft brush or cloth (do not wash !); cut into slices about 1/4 inch thick. Distribute these on a drying screen and place in your drier or out in the sun. Before storing, the mushrooms must be tinder dry.

To reconstitute dried mushrooms, soak them in boiling water for about half a minute, stirring as you soak them to loosen any dirt that may be present. Let the mushrooms and water set for a minute and a half and then lift them out gently with a slotted spoon and place on the chopping board. Some of the flavor will be in the water, so use no more water than necessary, and save it to use in your sauce. Dried mushrooms can be used in a variety of recipes, but they are most frequently used as flavoring agents only.

There are many books on mushrooms containing recipes. *Farmers Bulletin 796* has already been mentioned, as has McKenny and Stuntz's *The Savory Wild Mushroom.* Other books include Clyde Christensen's *Common Edible Mushrooms,* McIlvaine and MacAdam's *One Thousand American Fungi,* M.E. Hard's *The Mushroom,* and Helmut Ripperger's *Mushroom Cookery.* Nevertheless, chances are that you will end up using one or two of the simplest recipes almost exclusively. When you go out in the woods to collect mushrooms, bring along some matches so you can start a fire and be sure to have an onion and some butter with you. If you don't have a frying pan, find a green stick, split it open at one end, and place your mushroom in the cleft. Roast over the open fire, with or without a slice of onion next to it, and when tender, put a dab of butter on it and eat directly from the stick. If you are unlucky and don't find any mushrooms that day, well, you can always roast a slice of onion the same way.

mushroom identification keys

A botanical key is a simple device to aid in the identification, or recognition, of different kinds of plants. It consists of sets, usually pairs, of contrasting descriptive statements, called couplets, arranged in a series, with directions telling the user which set to go to next. By starting at the first choice, or couplet, and carefully following directions, one can identify any kind of plant for which the key was prepared. The chief advantage of the botanical key is that a large number of species can be identified by making only a small number of comparisons between the unknown plant in your hand and short descriptive statements. Each comparison eliminates, on the average, half of the remaining species. Consequently, over a thousand species can be separated and sorted out on the basis of an average of only ten comparisons; and four thousand species can be sorted, and all but one of them eliminated, by an average of twelve comparisons Thus, botanical keys are valuable time savers as we attempt to identify unknown species.

To identify means to recognize that an organism is the same as another organism which has previously been described. By "the same" we usually mean that the two belong to the same species; however, identification may be to any taxonomic group: Class, family, genus, or variety, for example. Some people tend to confuse the terms "identify" and "classify." Classification means that we have studied and worked out the genetic relationship of an organism, placing each species in its proper genus, family, and order. In this book, emphasis is on identification, but classification is frequently referred to because it aids in identification as well as helps us keep track of the large number of species that exist.

Emphasis in this book, up to now, has been on collecting mushrooms for food. But collecting mushrooms for table use is definitely not the only reason. People collect stamps, insects, wild flowers, leaves, and other objects just for the sake of having a properly identified set of specimens, or for aesthetic reasons, or to increase their scientific knowledge of biological materials. The keys in this chapter are useful to anyone wishing to build a herbarium of fungus materials for scientific studies, for photographic use, or other purposes. It is recommended that until you have gained considerable experience in keying mushrooms for herbarium use, you eat only those species described in chapters Two and Four.

Every key is limited. The keys in this chapter are limited to mushrooms and are of no value in identifying lichens, microscopic molds or other plants. They are also limited to North America and may be of little value if applied to mushrooms of other areas. While an attempt has been made to include every species of mushroom commonly found in this area, there are many omissions, due partly to our limited knowledge, especially of western mushrooms for which there is so much diversity and so few botanists who have studied them, and due partly to lack of space if we are to keep this book of a size that is useful and manageable. Some "lumping" has occurred in preparing the keys; where two or more species of poisonous mushrooms are so similar that it is difficult to distinguish among them, they are treated as a single species and given the name and edibility rating of the least desirable one. If an uncommon edible mushroom is very similar to a more common poisonous species, they may be lumped under the name and edibility rating of the poisonous species. Edibility ratings of lumped species are always those of the least desirable species in the group. The symbols used to indicate edibility are the same as those shown on page eight and used throughout the book: Stars (☆) indicate edibility and daggers (†) indicate toxicity.

Almost every key is limited in additional ways. Keys lead us to the right species by the process of elimination. If there are a hundred species included in a key and we make every choice correctly, we can be sure that our species is **not** one of the 99 that were eliminated; but we seldom can be really sure that it **is** the species whose name we have arrived at and not a species which somehow was not included in the key. It is likely, however, that our species will belong to the same genus as the species we reached in the key, and thus we have a clue that will simplify our task if we use one of the more technical books on mushroom identification. Another limitation of botanical keys is closely related to their chief advantage—their time saving value: If we make a wrong choice anywhere along the way in keying out a species, a misidentification is bound to occur. In the keys in this chapter, multiple statements are presented in most of the leads, in order that the user will more likely detect any errors he may have made in choosing between leads.

The couplets are numbered sequentially. Always begin with couplet no. 1 and then skip to whatever couplet is indicated; do not automatically go from no. 1 to no. 2 to no. 3 and so on. If there are several leads in a set (or couplet), read all of them before making the decision as to which one fits the mushroom in hand best. Sometimes, the first pair (or set) of statements cannot be utilized in making the decision; if so, go to the second pair (or set) in the same leads. If the mushroom seems to fit one statement of a lead but not the next one, either use the majority rule or attach greater weight to the first statement. Be very careful about "weasel words" like "usually," "sometimes," or "rarely." They are there because there is variation in every species which we need to be aware of, but they can cause confusion and uncertainty.

Eventually, instead of a number or key reference at the right hand margin there will be the name of a species. You have arrived! You have identified the specimen in hand! But check your specimen against the descriptive inform-ation given, and any pictures available, in case an incorrect choice was made somewhere along the way. If you are not satisfied with your final selection, work the key backwards, using the numbers in parentheses at the beginning of the first lead of each couplet, until you find a place where you may have made the wrong choice.

When collecting mushrooms for keying, it is good to have at least three specimens: Break or cut the cap off one and immediately begin a spore print, carefully dissect one right down through the center of the cap and stem for observation of gill attachment and other characteristics (see Fig. 3–7), and dry or otherwise preserve one for herbarium or reference purposes.

At each keying session, limit yourself to a few specimens. It is easy to collect 20 or 30 species of mushrooms in a short period of time when collecting conditions are good, but you will probably not be able to key out that many before some start to spoil. It would be better to collect four or five species and use the time for careful keying of those before collecting more.

On the following pages, there are six keys. The first is a general key to help you decide on the major group your mushroom belongs to; if you already know the major group (see Fig. 2, 4, 5, 6, 9 and 29), skip Key A and go to the specific key: Key B for the sac fungi (Ascomyceteae), C for the boletes and polypores, D for the chanterelles, tooth, and coral fungi, E for the puffballs, and F for the agarics or gill mushrooms. Species that might easily be misidentified in regard to their major group are included in more than one key.

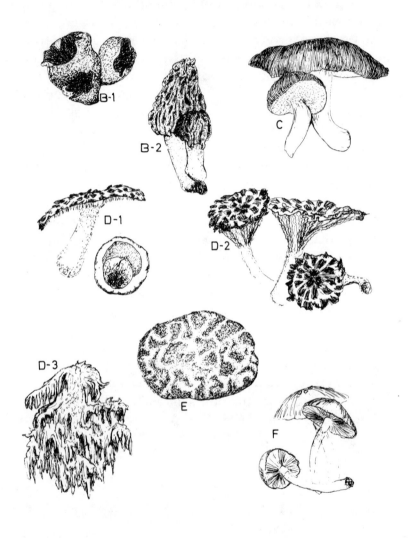

Fig. 29. Examples of the major groups of mushrooms; the letter by each illustration indicates the key in which it is found: **B-1.** *Peziza vesiculosa*, **B.-2** *Verpa bohemica*, **C.** *Suillus granulatus*, **D-1.** *Hydnum imbricatum*, **D-2.** *Cantharellus floccosus*, **D-3.** *Hericium caput-ursi*, **E.** *Calvatia booniana*, **F.** *Agaricus campestris*.

key a the major groups of mushrooms

1. Fruiting bodies having a definite cap and stem arrangement: the sporocarp may be umbrella shaped, with cap attached centrally to a long or short stem, or the cap may be eccentric, or resemble a sponge, saddle or other type of structure. . . **2**
1. Fruiting bodies not consisting of distinct cap and stem; sporocarps may resemble balls, cups, disks, clubs, or shelves **3**

2. Hymenium (spore-producing tissue) consisting of pits, wrinkles, or a smooth surface on the **upper** surface of the cap . . . . **key b,** p. 107
2. Hymenium consisting of pores or tubes on the **under** surface of the cap . . . . **key c,** p. 111
2. Hymenium consisting of tooth-like projections on the **under** surface of the cap . . . . **key d,** p. 119
2. Hymenium consisting of dichotomously branched veins and joined with cross-veins, on the **under** surface of the cap . . . . **key d,** p. 119
2. Hymenium consisting of gills (thin, wide plates with deep spaces between the adjacent plates) on the **under** surface of the cap . . . . **key f,** p. 136

3. Sporocarp a concave cup or flat plate or disk, sometimes convex, usually growing on soil, with spores produced on its **upper** surface. . . . . **key b,** p. 107
3. Sporocarp a flat shelf, or series of flat shelves, or a cap attached at its margin to a stump, log, or trunk, with spores produced on gills or in pores or tubes on the **under** surface of the cap. **4**
3. Sporocarp consisting of branched or unbranched clubs or spines, pointing up or down, with spores borne on the surface . . . . **key d,** p. 119
3. Sporocarp a ball or egg-like structure, usually on soil, with spores produced inside it. . . . . **key e,** p. 128

4. Undersurface of cap or shelves consisting of pores, the openings of tubes in which the spores are produced .... **key c,** p. 111
4. Undersurface of cap or shelves consisting of gills, or vertical flat plates, on which the spores are produced **key f,** p. 136

Throughout the book, edibility is indicated by these symbols (daggers for poisonous and stars for edible species):

†   – poisonous species

††   – deadly poisonous species

○   – undesirable but non-poisonous, or untested species

†○☆   – poisonous, but edible after parboiling

☆   – edible species

☆☆   – good species

☆☆☆   – choice species

○(☆)   – species that are edible but not recommended; easily confused with poisonous species

☆/†   – species ordinarily edible but poisonous under some conditions (*e.g.,* if consumed with alcohol or eaten raw)

☆/†○   – species probably edible but conflicting reports suggest caution

key b   the ascomyceteae or sac fungi

1. Sporocarps attached directly to the substratum without a stem **2**
1. Sporocarps consisting of distinct cap and stem **9**

2. (1) Fruiting body rather shapeless, forming a flat or convex brown crust on the soil, growing on burned over areas . . . . *Rhizina undulata* ○
2. Fruiting body extremely convex, the surface convoluted into brain-like ridges (Fig. 30) . . . . *Gyromitra gigas* ☆ ☆
2. Fruiting body concave or flat, disk or cup-like, not crustose **3**

3. (2) Cups many in a single rosette-like cluster (Fig. 30) . . . . *Peziza proteana* f. *sparassoides* ☆ ☆ ☆
3. Cups solitary to several, sometimes fused, but not rosette-like. **4**

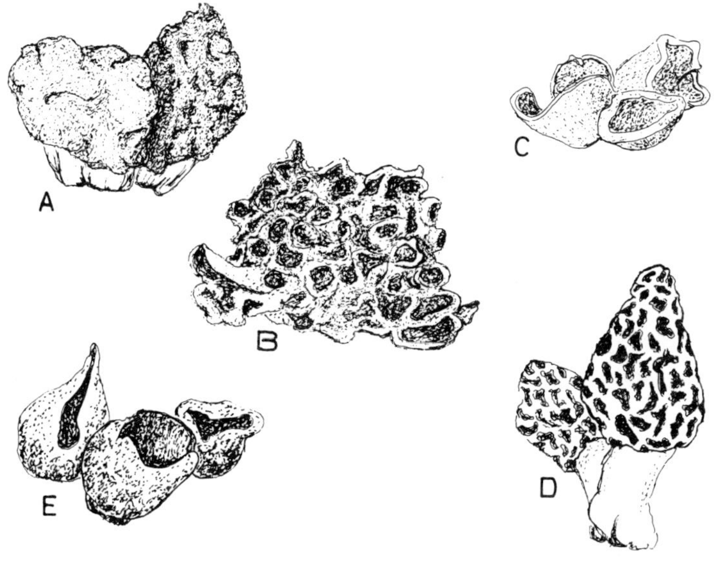

Fig. 30. Some ascomycetous mushrooms or sac fungi: **A.** *Gyromitra gigas,* **B.** *Peziza proteana* f. *sparassoides,* **C.** *Aleuria aurantica,* **D.** *Morchella deliciosa,* **E.** *Sarcosphaera coronaria.*

4. (3) Apothecium (fruiting body) flat, brown, with white rim (Fig. 4) . . . . *Discina ancilis* ☆☆
4. Apothecium cup-shaped, white, orange, or brown **5**

5. (4) Cups irregular in shape; orange in color **6**
5. Cups more or less regular in shape, with or without a broken margin; brown, cinnamon, or white in color 7

6. (5) With orange centers and margins, fruiting in fall (Fig. 30) . . . . *Aleuria aurantia* ☆☆
6. With orange centers and olive margins, fruiting in the spring . . . . *Caloscyphe fuelgens* ○

7. (5) Inside of cups pale brown, outside darker brown; growing on manure piles or heavily fertilized soil (Fig. 29) . . . . *Peziza vesiculosa* ☆☆
7. Inside of cups bluish or violet, outside white or gray; usually growing subterraneously (Fig. 30) *Sarcosphaera coronaria* †
7. Inside of cups cinnamon, outside pallid; growing under conifers or on conifer stumps. **8**

8. (7) Consistency jelly-like or rubbery; spores borne on basidia, not in sacs or asci; cups variable in shape, often deep and rounded; appearing in late summer, fall, or winter . . . . *Auricularia auricula* ○
8. Consistency firm; spores borne in cylindric sacs; cups shallow, saucer-like; appearing near snow banks in early spring. . . . . *Discina perlata* ○

9. (1) Caps smooth to slightly wrinkled, slightly reticulated, or bumpy on upper surface **10**
9. Caps wrinkled in tight vertical and convoluted ridges without cross walls joining the ridges **14**
9. Caps distinctly reticulated or pitted; horizontal cross walls joining the vertical walls. **16**

10. (9) Stems short, approximately as long as cap height; fruits usually umbrella-shaped with radiating ridges on undersurface of the caps (Fig. 19) .... *Helvella californica* †○ ☆

10. Stems long, about twice as long as cap height; caps usually saddle-shaped to disk-shaped, lacking ridges on undersurface **11**

10. Stems very long, several times as long as "cap" height; caps covered with foul-smelling green slime (see **key e,** couplet 17) . . . . stinkhorns ○

11. (10) With longitudinally ridged or fluted stems; caps usually distinctly saddle-shaped, pale yellowish to violet or light brown; stems similar but slightly lighter in color **12**

11. With smooth, non-fluted, pale pinkish stems and reddish brown, disk-shaped to saddle-shaped caps **13**

12. (11) Color of caps and stems pale yellow or sometimes off-white; stems relatively stout . . . . . . *Helvella crispa* ☆ ☆

12. Color of caps and stems smoky brown to purplish; stems relatively stout and distinctly fluted; common (Fig. 5) . . . . *Helvella lacunosa* †○ ☆ ☆

13. (11) Growing on well-rotted wood, sawdust or humus; stems always smooth; caps 3–25 cm. in diameter . . . . *Helvella infula* †○ ☆ ☆

13. Growing on damp soil in grassy areas in open woods; stems usually slightly fluted; caps 1–5 cm. in diameter . . . . *Helvella elastica* ☆ ☆

14. (9) Stems very short, sporocarps often appearing to be stemless; caps yellow-brown or darker (Fig. 30) . . . . *Gyromitra gigas* ☆ ☆

14. Stems about as long as height of caps; caps pink, tan or lighter **15**

15. (14) Wrinkling of caps very tight and twisted; caps and stems pink or flesh-colored (Fig. 19)

.... *Gyromitra esculenta* ††○ ☆ ☆ ☆

15. Wrinkling of caps rather loose; caps tan, stems lighter

.... *Gyromitra fastigiata* ☆ ☆ ☆

16. (9) Pits elongated; ridges vertical with less pronounced cross ridges forming the pits (Fig. 29) .... *Verpa bohemica* ☆ ☆

16. Pits squarish; both vertical and horizontal ridges prominent... **17**

17. (16) Margin of caps united to the stem.............. **18**

17. Margin of caps free from the stem................... **20**

18. (17) Caps rounded or oval, ridges and pits flesh colored to yellow-brown (Fig. 10) .... *Morchella esculenta* ☆ ☆ ☆

18. Caps oblong or cylindrical, ridges white, pits deep brown (Fig. 30)....................... *Morchella deliciosa* ☆ ☆

18. Caps conical or oblong conical, black or dark in color

.... **19**

19. (18) Base of cap the same diameter as or only slightly larger than the apex of the stem...... *Morchella angusticeps* ☆[1]

19. Base of cap distinctly larger than the apex of stem (Fig. 5) .... *Morchella conica* ☆[1]

20. (17) Stems free to middle of caps ... *Morchella semilibera* ☆

20. Stems free to apex of caps .... *Morchella bispora* ☆ ☆

1. Black morels are under suspicion; some people recommend parboiling them.

key C   the boletes and polypores

1. Individual tubes free, not united to each other
.... *Fistulina hepatica* ☆☆☆
1. Individual tubes united **2**

2. (1) Pore layer usually tough, thin, and firmly attached to caps; sporocarps usually lacking stems, attached laterally, stems, when present, often eccentric; spore print mostly white   **3**
2. Pore layer thick and succulent and usually easily separated from the cap; caps attached centrally to thick, fleshy stem; spore print usually brown, olive or yellow **10**

3. (2) Fruiting bodies fleshy, consisting of stems and caps; on soil.. **4**
3. Fruiting bodies woody, at least near attachment although margins may be fleshy, no true stems present; on logs, stumps or trees...................................... **5**

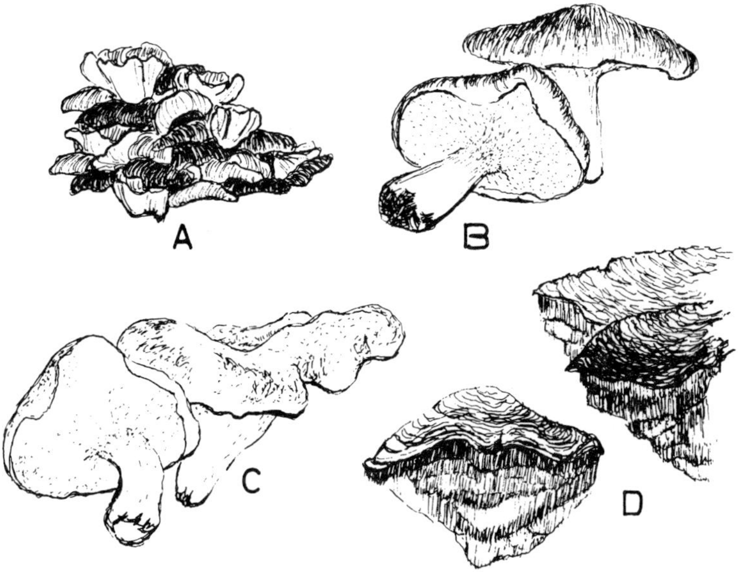

Fig. 31. Some bracket fungi and other polypores: **A.** *Polyporus frondosa,* **B.** *Polyporus leucomelas,* **C.** *Albatrellus ovinus,* **D.** *Fomes igniarius.*

4. (3) Top of caps more or less flat, margins wavy to undulating, caps white to creamy, often tinged with pink or violet tones (Fig. 31)......................... *Albatrellus ovinus* ☆☆

4. Top of caps plane to slightly convex, margins slightly wavy, mature caps dark brownish black (Fig. 31) .... *Polyporus leucomelas* ☆

4. Top of caps rounded to hemispherical, margins mostly smooth, caps tan to medium brown ...... *Albatrellus confluens* ☆

5. (3) Sporocarps consisting of single very woody shelves; tube layer stratified.. **6**

5. Sporocarps consisting of many overlapping, often fleshy shelves; tube layer single............................ **7**

6. (5) Caps flat to convex, much wider than high, growing on aspen and other deciduous trees (Fig. 31) *Fomes igniarius* ○

6. Caps hoof-like, much higher than wide, growing on conifers .... *Fomes officinalis* ○

7. (5) Gnarled, underground, stem-like structure present attaching the hard, woody shelves to base of a stump ....: *Osteina obducta* ○

7. Gnarled, underground, stem-like structures not present; attachment by short marginal stalks often high on stumps or logs; margins of shelves fleshy....................... **8**

8. (7) Tubes white; stems contain a milky latex .... *Polyporus cincinnatus* ○

8. Tubes colored; no milky latex in stems................. **9**

9. (8) Color of caps and pores sulfur yellow to orange brown (Fig. 14).................... *Polyporus sulphureus* ☆☆☆

9. Color of caps grayish brown, pores white (Fig. 31)...................... *Polyporus frondosa* ☆☆☆

9. Color of caps gray, violet, or other color .... *Polyporus griseus* or *P. flettii* ○

10. (2) Pores running down the stem; spores white (Fig. 31)
.... *Polyporus leucomelas* ☆

10. Pores only on undersurface of cap; spores colored... **11**

11. (10) Flesh of cap slowly turning violet gray when broken or bruised; caps bright red-orange (Fig. 32)
.... *Boletus aurantiacus* ☆☆☆

11. Flesh of cap or tube layer or base of stem turning blue when bruised or broken; caps mostly olive to grayish, not bright red-orange **12**

11. Flesh of cap, tube layer, and stem usually remaining white or yellow when broken or bruised, never staining blue or violet; caps usually yellow to chocolate, not bright red-orange **22**

12. (11) Mouths of tubes (pores) of mature caps red or scarlet **13**

12. Mouths of tubes of mature caps yellow, brown, or white, not red **14**

13. (12) Stems conspicuously bulbous, lower part red, upper olive like cap; caps dry; tubes greenish yellow when young becoming dark red at maturity (Fig. 32) ... *Boletus satanus* †

13. Stems slightly swollen at base, lower part pink, upper red; caps olive-brown and sticky when wet; tubes yellow with deep red mouths when young and when mature (Fig. 6)
.... *Boletus eastwoodii* †

14. (12) Caps of older specimens dry and cracked in a more or less rectangular pattern; flesh staining blue rapidly when broken... **15**

14. Caps viscid to slimy; if dry, not cracked in a rectangular pattern; flesh staining blue slowly when broken...... **18**

15. (14) With fine netting on stems; tubes lemon yellow with greenish cast; caps not velvety........ *Boletus calopus* †

15. Without netting on stems; tubes yellowish without greenish cast; caps velvety **16**

16. (15) Stems stout, typically 4–5 cm. in diameter by 8–10 cm. long; caps olive-bluff .... *Boletus rubripes* ○
16. Stems slender, typically 1—1.5 cm. in diameter by 6—8 cm. long; caps olive-gray to olive-brown, not olive-buff... **17**

17. (16) Spore print dark wood brown; cap olive-brown; stems brown; flavor bitter............... *Boletus amylosporus* †
17. Spore print dark olive; cap olive gray; stems browish with red areas; flavor mild.... *Boletus porosporus* var. *americanus* ☆☆

18. (14) Pores dark coffee brown; flesh staining first blue, then brown .... *Boletus pseudoscaber* ☆
18. Pores yellow to pale brown; flesh staining blue only..... **19**

19. (18) Stems yellow for entire length, covered with brownish or reddish dots or else having a ring; flavor mild and pleasant.. **20**
19. Stems at least partly red, smooth, neither dotted nor having a ring; flavor either bitter or practically tasteless **21**

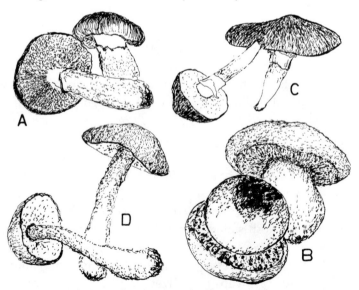

Fig. 32. Some edible and poisonous boletes: **A.** *Boletus aurantiacus*, the orange-cap bolete; **B.** *Boletus satanus*; **C.** *Boletus coerulescens*, the blue-staining bolete; **D.** *Suillus cavipes*.

20. (19) Annulus or ring lacking; stems glandular dotted; flesh of cap staining blue .... *Boletus hirtellus* ☆
20. Annulus or ring present; stems smooth above and below ring; only base of stem staining blue (Fig. 32)
.... *Boletus coerulescens* ☆

21. (19) Base as well as apex of stem red; cap blackish brown
.... *Boletus zelleri* ☆☆
21. Base of stem yellow, apex red; cap reddish with yellow margin .... *Boletus smithii* ○

22. (11) Upper surface of caps covered with small fibrillose scales; dry ring present near apex of stem, base of stem staining pea green when cut .... *Suillus lakei* ☆☆
22. Upper surface of caps covered with coarse cottony patches; thin ring present on robust specimens; base of stem staining vinaceous where handled, old stems mostly hollow
.... *Suillus sibiricus* ○
22. Upper surface of caps slimy or dry but not covered with scales or patches of veil tissue; ring present or absent; base of stem and other flesh remaining white or yellow... **23**

23. (22) Having glandular dotted stems................. **24**
23. Having netted or reticulate stems................... **30**
23. Having smooth stems with neither glandular dots nor nets present... **35**

24. (23) Ring present on stem......................... **25**
24. Ring absent **27**

25. (24) Annulus or ring broad, slimy, and prominent.... **26**
25. Annulus or ring narrow, dry, obscure or absent on some specimens... **29**

26. (25) Flavor acid; cap yellow to buff; pores brown
.... *Suillus acidus* ☆☆
26. Flavor mild, pleasant, but not acid; cap olive to brown; pores yellow **28**

27. (24) Base of stem tapered slightly, stems solid; caps slimy but do not appreciably stain the hands; tubes honey yellow, brownish in age; stems white with cinnamon base and cap; ring absent (Fig. 29) .... *Suillus granulatus* ☆☆

27. Base of stem slightly bulbous, stems hollow, caps slimy and stain the hands yellow; tubes mustard yellow, yellow-brown in age; stems yellow covered with reddish dots; ring may be present on robust specimens.... *Suillus americanus* ☆☆

28. (26) Outer edge of ring yellow, slimy; inner part of ring brownish, dry; caps olive to vinaceous brown; stems conspicuously glandular dotted (Fig. 21) *Suillus subolivaceous* ☆☆

28. Outer edge of ring purple-brown, slimy; inner part of ring yellow, slimy; caps slimy, brown; stems slightly dotted .... *Suillus luteus* ☆☆

29. (25) Caps brown to olive, sticky when wet but do not stain hands appreciably; stems dotted greenish brown .... *Suillus subluteus* ☆☆

29. Caps yellow, sticky, stain hands yellow when handled; stems dotted cinnamon to reddish brown .... *Suillus americanus* ☆☆

30. (23) With brown to blackish tufts of hair on the stems; caps white becoming gray-brown to yellow-brown .... *Boletus scaber* ☆☆☆

30. Without tufts of hair on stems; caps tan to brown ... **31**

31. (30) Stems stout, short (mostly < 10 cm.), distinctly bulbous; caps 10–20 cm. or more in diameter, dry, brown; tubes white, becoming greenish yellow in age (Fig. 20) .... *Boletus edulis* ☆☆☆

31. Stems slender to stout, relatively long (mostly > 10 cm.) tapered to slightly bulbous; caps mostly 5–10 cm. diameter, sometimes more; tubes yellow to brown, not greenish yellow... **32**

32. (31) The caps dark blackish brown **33**
32. The caps yellow to gray, sometimes with greenish patches **34**

33. (32) Tubes coffee brown ... *Boletus olivaceobrunneus* ☆☆☆
33. Tubes white to pale tan .... *Boletus aureus* ☆☆☆

34. (32) Annulus slimy with orange outer ring; pores large, slightly decurrent; flavor mild .... *Boletus immitatus* ☆
34. Annulus absent; pores white turning pink; flavor bitter
.... *Boletus felleus* ○

35. (23) Remnants of veil attached to margin of cap leaving lilac brown to chocolate patches; stems white (Fig. 22)
.... *Suillus borealis* ☆☆☆
35. Remnants of veil not present, or if present, not leaving colored patches; stems usually yellow to brown...... **36**

36. (35) Pores on undersurface of cap small with thick, fleshy walls, the pores randomly arranged.................. **37**
36. Pores large or coarse with thin, membranous walls, the pores often radially alligned **39**

37. (36) Caps moist but not viscid, dull yellow to reddish
.... *Boletus subglabripes* ☆
37. Caps sticky or slimy, cinnamon to chestnut brown ... **38**

38. (37) Ring present; stem bright yellow, turning brownish with age .... *Boletus elegans* ☆☆
38. Ring absent; stem yellowish brown ... *Boletus flaviporus* ☆

39. (36) Flesh white, soft; caps dry with reddish hairs (Fig. 32)
.... *Suillus cavipes* ☆☆☆
39. Flesh pink just under the cortex, yellow beneath; caps dry with reddish hairs........... *Suillus ochracearoseus* ☆☆
39. Flesh yellow; caps glabrous or scaly, dry to moist **40**

40. (39) Stems with prominent woolly ring; color of caps variable, mostly russet to chestnut with dingy yellow margins; base of stem slowly turning blue where broken or bruised (Fig. 32) .... *Boletus coerulescens* ☆

40. Stems lacking rings or with obscure rings; color of caps yellow to brown with margins as dark as rest of cap; no part of plant staining blue when broken or bruised **41**

41. (40) Surface of caps rough scaly, caps yellow to reddish brown; pores brownish................ *Suillus lakei* ☆☆

41. Surface of caps glabrous, buff with brown spots; pores large, mustard yellow to yellow-brown ..... *Suillus sibiricus* ○

Fig. 33. Some common chanterelles: **A.** *Cantharellus infundibulum;* **B.** *Craterellus cornucopioides,* **C.** *Clitocybe illudens,* the jack o'lantern mushroom or false chanterelle; **D.** *Cantharellus subalbidus.* Note the blunt gills, or veins, rather than sharp gills, and the connecting cross veins in the true chanterelles as opposed to *Clitocybe.*

key d   chanterelles, coral, & tooth fungi

1. Spores borne on veins on the undersurface of a more or less trumpet shaped cap, or undersurface that is smooth or nearly so. **2**
1. Spores borne on the surface of downward-pointing projections resembling teeth, either on the undersurface of caps or on the branches of a massive structure lacking a stem **10**
1. Spores borne on the surface of upward-pointing club-like or coral-like projections or a jelly-like structure **20**

2. (1) Cap distinctly funnel-shaped with arched margin; mature caps with a hole in the center leading into the hollow stem; caps tan to brown or brownish gray (Fig. 33) . . . . *Cantharellus infundibuliformis* ☆
2. Cap usually funnel-shaped with entire to wavy but not arched margin; caps lacking hole in center; white to orange, red, yellow, or purple **3**

3. (2) Undersurface and sometimes upper surface of caps purple **4**
3. Undersurface and sometimes upper surface of caps yellow, red, or white **6**

4. (3) Veins lacking except near the margin; flesh thin, brittle, dingy brown (Fig. 33) . . . . *Craterellus cornucopioides* ☆ ☆ ☆
4. Veins twisted or wrinkle-like, extending almost to base of stem **5**
4. Veins prominent, mostly straight, extending half way down stem (Fig. 5) . . . . *Cantharellus tubaeformis* ○

5. (4) Flesh soft, thick, blue-black; caps and veins deep purple . . . . *Cantharellus multiplex* ☆ ☆
5. Flesh firm white or tinged cinnamon; caps and veins pale violet to faded purplish brown . . . . *Cantharellus clavatus* ☆ ☆

6. (3) Upper surface of caps covered with scales; margins of caps entire, not wavy; veins twisted, wrinkle-like........ **7**

6. Upper surface of caps glabrous, not scaly; margins of caps usually wavy or lobed; veins more or less gill-like..... **8**

7. (6) Scales on caps red to dull orange (Fig. 29)
.... *Cantharellus floccosus* †

7. Scales on caps fire red; caps small..... *Cantharellus bonari* †

7. Scales on caps clay colored to tawny olive
.... *Cantharellus kaufmannii* †

8. (6) Color a uniform orange over caps, gills, and stem; cap slightly depressed with an umbo at its center, margin entire or slightly ragged; fruits luminescent; gills relatively wide, lacking crossveins; growing in clusters on rotting wood (Fig. 33) .... *Clitocybe illudens*[1] †

8. Color egg yellow to white with stem and undersurface of caps lighter than upper surface; caps slightly to deeply depressed, no umbo present, margin lobed to wavy; gills or veins shallow, connected by crossveins; sporocarps not luminescent, usually growing singly.. **9**

9. (8) Margin of caps wavy, caps egg yellow on upper surface, cream colored below; cross veins pronounced (Fig. 26)
.... *Cantharellus cibarius* ☆☆☆

9. Margin of caps lobed, caps white, staining rusty yellow to orange where injured; stems short, stocky (Fig. 33)
.... *Cantharellus subalbidus* ☆☆☆

10. (1) Sporocarps massive, attached by margins to trees or stumps... **11**

10. Sporocarps consisting of cap and stem, usually growing on soil... **13**

1. *Clitocybe illudens* is also known as *Omphalotus olearus* and *Cantharellus aurantiaca*; care must be taken to avoid confusing it with *Cantharellus cibarius*.

11. (10) Texture of fruit woody; caps conk-like, hoof-shaped with rough, cracked upper surface and teeth tightly crowded on undersurface .... *Echinodontium tinctorum* ○

11. Texture of fruit fleshy, moist; not conk-like; teeth not crowded **12**

12. (11) Teeth less than 1.5 cm. long; axis much branched (Fig. 28) .... *Hericium coraloides* ☆☆

12. Teeth greater than 1.5 cm. long; axis slightly branched (Fig. 29) .... *Hericium caput-ursi* ☆☆

13. (10) Fruiting bodies small (1–3 cm. broad); caps attached laterally to the substrate by marginal stems.......... **14**

13. Fruiting bodies larger (2–30 cm. broad); caps attached centrally.. **15**

14. (13) Sporocarps gelatinous with a whitish translucent appearance; never growing on pine cones
.... *Pseudohydnum gelatinosum* ☆

14. Sporocarps not gelatinous or translucent, caps brown and hairy, growing on pine cones (Fig. 34)
.... *Auriscalpium vulgare* ○

15. (13) Color of cap uniformly salmon pink to reddish, smooth to slightly scaly; spines white or buff; flavor mild (Fig. 27)
.... *Hydnum repandum* ☆☆☆

15. Color of cap, stem, and spines uniformly purple; caps slightly scaly; flavor very faint, resembling cinnamon
.... *Hydnum fuscoindicum* ☆

15. Color of cap uniformly cream or tan to dull brown; caps smooth to distinctly scaly or woolly; spines mostly grayish brown to cinnamon brown; flavor mild, bitter, or peppery **16**

15. Color of cap not uniform; dark brown in center and white to salmon pink on margins or in bands of alternating lighter and darker zones.................................... **18**

16. (15) Upper surface of cap smooth (Fig. 34)
.... *Hydnum umbilicatum* ☆☆
16. Upper surface of cap scaly or woolly **17**

17. (16) Spines grayish brown with lilac tinge; stems, including base, grayish buff; flavor mild, pleasant (Fig. 29)
.... *Hydnum imbricatum* ☆
17. Spines grayish brown; stems buff with blackish green base; flavor bitter...................... *Hydum scabrosum* ○
17. Spines brown with light tips; stems dingy orange brown, felted; flavor and odor unpleasantly sweet
.... *Hydnellum aurantiacum* ○

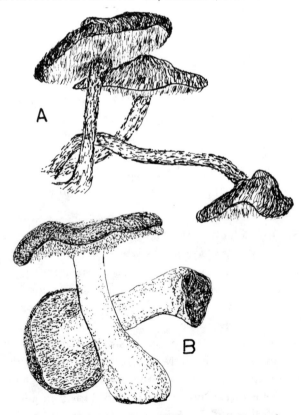

Fig. 34. Two species of toothed mushrooms: **A.** *Auriscalpium vulgare* and **B.** *Hydnum umbilicatum.*

18. (15) Caps and stems very tough and woody, the surface of the caps strongly marked with concentric rings of brown and black, the margins white; spore print white

.... *Phellodon tomentosum* ○

18. Caps and stems fleshy or stems woody with age, caps dark brown in center and pale salmon pink on margins, or cinnamon brown with narrow, darker concentric rings; spores brown... **19**

19. (18) Blood red drops of liquid exuded from fruits in wet weather; surface of caps covered with course nodules; spines salmon pink to brown .... *Hydnum peckii* ○

19. Blood red drops of liquid not exuded from fruits; scattered brown scales on cap; spines rusty cinnamon

.... *Hydnum stereocarcinon* ○

20. (1) Sporocarps unbranched, club-like to more or less cup-like **21**

20. Sporocarps branched into finger-like or coral-like structures

.... **28**

21. (20) Consistency of fruiting body like stiff, rubbery gelatin or sometimes like soft gelatin **22**

21. Consistency of fruiting body firm, fleshy **25**

22. (21) Fruiting bodies with stalks, funnel shaped, growing on soil; pink to rose; firm gelatinous

.... *Phlogiotis helvelloides* ☆☆

22. Fruiting bodies without stalks, ear-like, cup-like, or more or less shapeless; orange to brown; growing on wood... **23**

23. (22) The sporocarps brown, ear-shaped, often wrinkled, tough and rubbery-gelatinous when dry.............. **24**

23. The sporocarps yellow to orange lobed masses, not wrinkled, soft gelatinous to tough and horny when dry **24**

24. (23) Surface convoluted into a yellow brain-like structure; fruits large (2–10 cm.), horny when dry
.... *Tremella mesenterica* ○
24. Surface lobed; sporocarps red-orange, small (1–6 cm.), usually many in a group, collapse when dry
.... *Dacrymyces palmatus* ☆

25. (21) Apex of sporocarp covered with green slime; odor fetid and very disagreeable (See Key E, couplet 17)
.... stinkhorns ○
25. Apex of sporocarp not covered with slime, same color as rest of sporocarp; odor not fetid or especially unpleasant
.... **26**

26. (25) Sporocarps broadly club-shaped, flattened at apex
.... **27**
26. Sporocarps narrowly club-shaped, not flattened
.... *Clavaria ligula* ☆

27. (26) Flavor bitter (Fig. 9)............ *Clavaria borealis* ☆
27. Flavor pleasant..................... *Clavaria truncata* ☆

28. (20) Tips of branches flattened, branches crowded into a cabbage-like rosette................................. **29**
28. Tips of branches not flattened, branches few to many, sometimes crowded but not cabbage-like in appearance
.... **30**

29. (28) Color white to pale yellow (Fig. 35)
.... *Sparassis radicata* ☆☆☆
29. Color pinkish to tan with lilac at base of rosette
.... *Peziza proteana* ☆☆

30. (28) Branches short with knobby purplish tips
.... *Ramaria botrytis* ☆☆☆
30. Branches long, neither knobby nor purplish tipped... **31**

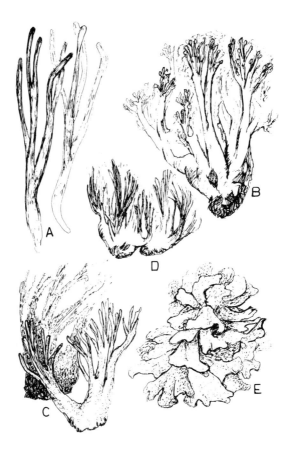

Fig. 35. Examples of coral fungi: **A.** *Calocera viscora,* **B.** *Ramaria brunnea,* **C.** *Ramaria sanguinea,* **D.** *Ramaria formosa,* **E.** *Sparassis radicata.* A poisonous species, *R. gelatinosa,* is almost identical in outward appearance to *R. formosa* but has a translucent, jelly-like interior at the base.

31. (30) Fruiting bodies flesh colored to salmon-pink; spore print yellow to ocher; on humus or soil **32**

31. Fruiting bodies yellow; spore print yellow to ocher; usually on rotting logs **33**

31. Fruiting bodies white to ivory, often tinged with violet; spore print white; on soil or wood **37**

32. (31) Base of cluster when cut open gelatinous in the center; spore fruits cream colored to pinkish cinnamon, flesh creamy white to pink, not staining brown to black when bruised or broken; spore print ocher.......... *Ramaria gelatinosa* †

32. Base of cluster not gelatinous inside; spore fruits salmon to rosy pink, flesh white turning cinnamon brown or black when bruised; spore print yellow (Fig. 35) *Ramaria formosa* ☆/†○

33. (31) The base of the sporocarp is only slightly larger in diameter than the branches; branches few (typically 5–15); growing on wood (Fig. 35)......... *Calocera viscorsa* ○

33. The base of the sporocarp much larger in diameter than the branches; branches many (typically 20–60); on wood or duff **34**

34. (33) Growing on rotting logs; flesh white, soft, not changing color when bruised or broken; spore print yellow.... **35**

34. Growing on duff under conifers; flesh when bruised or broken turning vinaceous red; spore print ocherous **36**

35. (34) Flavor mild, pleasant............. *Ramaria flava* ☆

35. Flavor bitter (Fig. 9) .... *Ramaria stricta* ○

36. (34) Sporocarp rusty yellow, cut surfaces changing to vinaceous and then brown; taste bitter (Fig. 35) .... *Ramaria brunnea* ○

36. Sporocarp pale yellow, cut surfaces changing to vinaceous red and remaining red; taste pleasant, mild (Fig. 35) ....*Ramaria sanguinea* ☆☆

37. (31) Growing on the ground; sparingly branched .... *Ramaria cristata* ☆☆☆

37. Growing on wood; profusely branched with crown-like branch tips .... *Ramaria pyxidata* ☆☆☆

key e puffballs and similar fungi

1. Flesh of dissected sporocarps heterogeneous, having differentiated layers of tissue such as partly developed gills, etc., which are readily observable when the sporocarps are split longitudinally from top to bottom..................2
1. Flesh of dissected sporocarps homogeneous; when sporocarps are split longitudinally, the interior is uniformly firm and white
   .... **4**

2. (1) Interior of the egg-like sporocarp a fully developed, foul smelling, rubbery structure covered with green slime containing mature spores; no external stalk present; when fully mature, the internal structure elongates into a phallus-like stalk by rupturing the "egg"...................... **17**
2. Interior of the sporocarp an embryonic stem and cap with well developed gills or pores beginning to form; spores not yet developed; no external stalk visible (Fig. 12)
   .... button stage agaric[1]
2. Interior of the sporocarp consisting of a columella, or undeveloped stem, and much wrinkled or poorly developed gill-like structures; stalk usually present.................. **3**

3. (2) Sporocarp white, narrow parabolic to cylindrical, with "shaggy" tufts of hair-like scales; found only on deserts, mostly warm deserts, and dry tropical sites
   .... *Podaxis pistillaris* ○
3. Sporocarps white to yellow, pink, or purplish, spheroidal, with rhizomorphs often present but not scales; found in coniferous forests, lawns, or grassy meadows in temperate sites **18**

4. (1) Outer sporocarp wall splits into about 5 or 6 segments which curve back to form the rays of an "earth star" **5**
4. Outer sporocarp wall remains intact and fused to inner wall 7

1. Among the agarics sometimes mistaken for puffballs are *Amanita virosa* ††, *Amanita muscaria* †, *Agaricus campestris* ☆☆☆, and *Pholiota hiemalis* †.

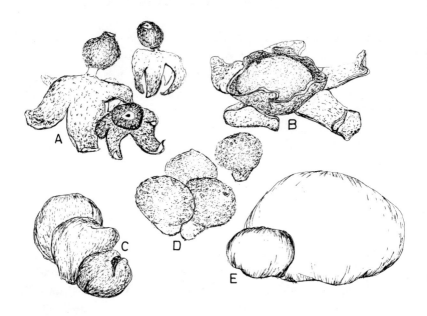

Fig. 36. Examples of earthstars and puffballs: **A.** *Geastrum coronatum;* **B.** *Geastrum triplex;* **C.** *Scleroderma bovista,* the pigskin puffball or false puffball; **D.** *Lycoperdon pyriforme;* **E.** *Calvatia gigantea.*

5. (4) Rays open up when wet, close up around the spore sac when dry; spore sac hairy...... *Astreus hygrometricus* ○
5. Rays remain open when dry; spore sac smooth **6**

6. (5) Inner spore sac on a short stalk; no "bowl" present (Fig. 36)....................... *Geastrum coronatum* ○
6. Inner spore sac not stalked; spore sac seated in a "bowl" (Fig. 36)........................... *Geastrum triplex* ○

7. (4) Fruiting body resembling a miniature bird's nest with several spore sacs enclosed in a single outer wall
....*Cyathus striatus* ○
7. Fruiting body not like a bird's nest, only one spore sac enclosed within the outer wall....................... **8**

8. (7) Gleba (spore-producing tissue) firm to hard, not spongy, purple to purplish brown, or sporocarp hollow with purple inner surface of inner wall; outer wall usually thick ...   **9**

8. Gleba fleshy, firm, and spongy; white (yellowish to brown in older specimens); outer wall usually thin, not purple....   **10**

9. (8) Growing as a hollow sphere just below the soil surface .... *Sarcosphaera eximia*   ☆☆

9. Growing as a firm, sometimes slightly irregular mass at the base of a stump or tree or on the ground (Fig. 36) .... *Scleroderma bovista*   †

10. (8) Spores discharged through an operculum, or opening at the apex of the fruiting body, in a bellows fashion; sporocarps mostly small (7–8 cm.), not stalked.................   **11**

10. Spores discharged by breaking of the upper part of the sporocarp, no operculum present; sporocarps mostly medium to large (5–60 cm.), often stalked...........   **14**

11. (1) Sporocarps round or oval, white **12**

11. Sporocarps pear shaped, white to light brown **13**

12. (11) Outer skin chalky white, covered with small, pointed warts; sporocarps small (1–4.5 cm.)   *Lycoperdon candida* ☆

12. Outer skin dull white, smooth; sporocarps very small (0.8–2.0 cm., Fig. 11) ....   *Lycoperdon pusillum*   ○

13. (11) Brown pigments present; outer skin light brown and smooth; sporocarps small (0.5–4.5 cm.); on wood (Fig. 36) .... *Lycoperdon pyriforme*   ☆☆☆

13. Brown pigments absent; outer skin dull white, covered with pointed spines; small to medium (3–7 cm.); on soil (Fig. 6) .... *Lycoperdon perlatum*   ☆☆☆

14. (10). Found under conifers in the mountains, usually in the spruce-fir zone; skin covered with flat or sometimes slightly pointed warts; fruits small to medium (5–15 cm.)....   **15**

14. Found in lawns and grassy areas or in wet fields or along drainage ditches; skin smooth or covered with flat to slightly pointed warts; fruits medium to large (6–50 cm.) **16**

14. Found in arid habitats: Old corrals, dry slopes, or near sagebrush; fruits covered with large, flat warts with slightly darker centers; fruits large (40–60 cm.)

.... *Calvatia booniana* ☆☆☆

15. (14) Warts small (8–15 mm. across), dark, permanent; fruits solitary, small to medium (6–10 cm.) *Calvatia subcretacea* ☆

15. Warts large (25–40 mm. across), gray, deciduous; fruits solitary to gregarious, medium (6–16 cm.)

.... *Calvatia subsculpta* ☆

16. (14) Fruits large (20–60 cm.); common in lowlands (Fig. 36)....................... *Calvatia gigantea* ☆☆☆

16. Fruits smaller (6–16 cm.); common in mountains (Fig. 11)
.... *Calvatia subsculpta* ☆

17. (2) Head present; smooth, green slimy *Phallus ravenellii* ○

17. Head present; wrinkled to reticulate, green, slimy (Fig. 37)
.... *Phallus impudicus* ○

17. Head absent; the stem tapering to a narrow tip covered with a green slime (Fig. 37).............. *Mutinus caninus* ○

18. (3) Skin white at first, becoming buff to dingy brown; flesh white at first, becoming pale brown; stalk more or less fibrous, total aspect of sporocarp similar to an unexpanded *Agaricus;* found in lawns or grassy meadows; odor pleasant
............................*Endoptychum agaricoides* ☆☆

18. Skin white, not darkening with age or where bruised; flesh chocolate to black; stalk more or less fibrous and aspect similar to an unexpanded *Agaricus;* usually found under aspen or lodgepole pine; odor disagreeable
................................*Endoptychum depressum* ○

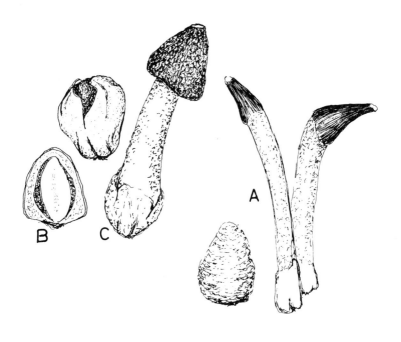

Fig. 37. Examples of stinkhorns: **A.** *Mutinus caninus,* mature sporocarp; **B.** *Phallus impudicus* "egg;" **C.** *Phallus impudicus,* mature sporocarp.

18. Skin olive, pink, or purplish, or a combination of these colors; flesh ocherous consisting of convoluted "gills"; stalk short and exceedingly fragile as in *Russula;* found mostly under spruce and fir; odor pleasant *Macowanites americanus* ☆

18. Skin white to yellow, quickly changing to rosy red where bruised; flesh white staining red where cut, becoming olive to cinnamon brown as the spores mature, spongy or rubbery; stalk absent, sporocarps usually buried in duff under pine or douglas fir; odor mild, almond like
.... *Rhizopogon rubescens* ○

TABLE I
synopsis of
stature characteristics and spore color of gill mushrooms

†† indicate genera in which deadly poisonous species are known to occur;
other poisonous genera are not indicated.

Where a genus is listed under more than one category, the rare or unusual types are indicated by parentheses.

STATURE TYPE		COLOR OF SPORE PRINT				
major categories	minor categories	white, pale lilac, pale yellow	pink, salmon, reddish	rusty or clear, brown or olive	smoky or purplish brown	black
	both ring and volva present	Amanita †† (Armillaria)		Clarkeinda Rozites		
	volva present but no ring	(Amanita ††)	Volvariella		(Agaricus)	Coprinus
FREE OR FINELY ATTACHED GILLS	ring present but no volva	Lepiota Limacella Chlorophyllum (Amanita ††)	Chameota	(Chlorophyllum)	Agaricus	Coprinus
	neither ring nor volva present	Russula (Amanita ††) (Hygrophorus) (Lepiota)	Pluteus	Pluteolus (Bolbitius) (Conocybe)	(Agaricus)	Coprinus Panaeolus

gills adnexed to adnate; no ring or volva present	Clitocybe Hygrophorus Laccaria Lactarius Lyophyllum Russula Tricholoma	Entoloma ✝✝	Cortinarius Hebeloma Inocybe Paxillus Pholiota (Agrocybe) (Naucoria)	Hypholoma Naematoloma	
ATTACHED GILLS AND FLESHY FIBROUS, THICK STEMS gills decurrent, no ring or volva present	Cantharellus Clitocybe Hygrophorus Lactarius Omphalotus Russula	Clitopilus	Paxillus (Inocybe) (Pholiota)		Chroogomphus Gomphidius
gills variable, ring present, no volva	Armillaria Cystoderma Lentinus (Amanita ✝✝)		Gymnopilus Hebeloma Pholiota Rozites (Inocybe)	Hypholoma Stropharia	Chroogomphus Gomphidius

synopsis of stature characteristics and spore color of gill mushrooms; cont.

major categories	minor categories	white, pale lilac, pale yellow	pink, salmon, reddish	rusty or clear, brown or olive	smoky or purplish brown	black
	gills adnexed to adnate; no ring or volva present	Collybia Marasmius Mycena	Leptonia †† Nolanea †† (Entoloma ††)	Agrocybe Bolbitius Naucoria Phaeocollybia (Galerina ††) (Inocybe)	Psathyrella Psilocybe (Panaeolus)	Coprinus Panaeolus Psathyrella
ATTACHED GILLS & THIN, TOUGH CARTILAGINOUS STEMS	gills decurrent, no ring or volva present	Marasmius Omphalina	(Leptonia ††)	Tubaria	(Psilocybe)	
	gills variable, ring present, no volva	(Mycena)		Conocybe Galerina ††	Psilocybe	Coprinus Panaeolus Psathyrella
	gills split longitudinally	Schizophyllum				
CAP TO STEM ATTACHMENT ECCENTRIC, OR MARGINAL WITH OR WITHOUT A STEM	gills not split	Lentinus Lenzites Panus Pleurotus Plicatura	Claudopus	Paxillus Crepidotus		

key f the gill mushrooms

The gill mushrooms are relatively difficult to identify:
The distinguishing characteristics are not as clearly defined
as the in the previous groups, intergrading types seem to
be more common, and the extremely large number of
species present difficult problems. Since the most powerful
toxins known among the fungi are found in the gill
mushrooms, and are relatively widespread, these keys
should be used primarily for tentative identification for
herbarium use or to confirm identification in groups in
which you are already well acquainted. Remember, if you
are not 100% positive of identification, either consult a
specialist for help, throw the mushroom away, or donate it
to a fungus herbarium; but do not eat it!

To identify gill mushrooms, spore print color, stature
type, and gill attachment are especially important. If you
have already ascertained the spore color, go directly to the
keys to the different spore prints:

> White, yellowish, greenish, or pale lilac spores,
>> No. 27, page 140.
>
> Pink, salmon, or flesh-brown spores,
>> No. 94, page 153.
>
> Brown, yellowish brown, clay brown, or cinnamon
>> spores, No. 102, page 155.
>
> Purple-brown to chocolate brown spores,
>> No. 141, page 164.
>
> Smoky-gray to black spores, No. 161, page 167.

If you have problems, consult Table 1 for help in
finding the right genus or to confirm your identification.
After identifying your mushroom, read the genus descriptions in Chapter Six for further confirmation.

1. Attachment of stem to cap central..................... **2**
1. Attachment of stem to cap eccentric, or cap attached to a
stump or log by its margin without a stem........... **26**

2. (1) Gills white or whitish, free from stem (see Fig. 3, p. 27)
.... **3**
2. Gills attached to stem or, if free, not whitish........... **8**

3. (2) Volva and annulus both present, the volva consisting of
either a series of ring-like markings or a distinct cup; it may
be underground so care must be taken in picking the sporocarp.. **33**
3. Volva present, annulus absent........................ **4**
3. Volva absent, annulus may or may not be present...... **5**

4. (3) Mature gills white, volva white and cup-like; spore print
white; mushrooms of bogs, especially in east U.S.
.................................*Amanita fulva* ○(☆)
4. Mature gills gray to black, volva a series of black threads
or scales terminating in a wavy basal zone; spore print
black; mushrooms of lawns and roadsides, common (Fig. 38)
.... *Coprinus atramentarius* ☆☆/†

5. (3) Annulus present.................................. **6**
5. Annulus absent..................................... **7**

6. (5) Base of stem swollen as in the Amanitas; gills white
turning cream at maturity; cap viscid (sticky); annulus a
wide ring which may slide up and down the stem... **38**
6. Base of stem tapered; gills pale or flesh colored turning
dark brown to black at maturity; cap usually dry; annulus
obscure to prominent but not a ring that can slide on
the stem.. **142**

7. (5) Spore print white; gills yellowish, blackening where
bruised, waxy appearance and feeling (Fig. 38)
.................................*Hygrophorus conicus* ○

7. Spore print pink or rose colored, often very pale pink; gills usually flesh-colored to salmon, not changing color **97**
7. Spore print brown; cap and gills usually some shade of brown **105**
7. Spore print purple brown; gills flesh-colored turning chocolate brown with age (Fig. 29) . . . *Agaricus campestris* ☆☆☆
7. Spore print black; gills gray to black turning inky or becoming shriveled with age . . . . *Coprinus plicatilis* ○

8. (2) Milky latex exuded where a young stem or cap is broken **44**
8. Milky latex not present **9**

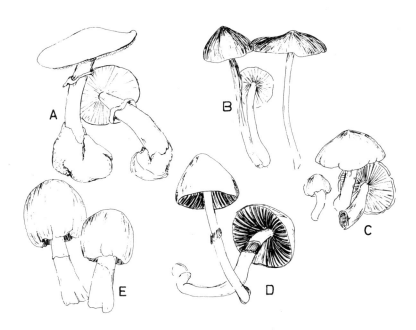

Fig. 38. Examples of mushrooms that can be identified without the aid of a spore print: **A.** *Amanita verna;* **B.** *Hygrophorus conicus;* **C.** *Hypholoma appendiculata,* **D.** *Panaeolus separatus;* **E.** *Coprinus atramentarius.* *A. verna* differs from other deadly poisonous *Amanitas* in minute stem and cap characteristics, odor, and spore details.

9. (8) Stems thick, brittle, snapping like a piece of chalk **54**

9. Stems thick (mostly > 5 mm.) and fleshy fibrous but not brittle... **10**

9. Stems thin (mostly < 5 mm.), tough, and cartilaginous **20**

10. (9) Annulus or ring present......................... **11**

10. Annulus or ring absent **12**

11. (10) Spore print white............................. **66**

11. Spore print brown................................. **125**

11. Spore print purple-brown.......................... **148**

11. Spore print black................................. **165**

12. (10) The gill attachment adnexed to adnate or sinuate **13**

12. The gill attachment decurrent or arcuate............ **17**

13. (12) Gills waxy feeling when a piece of material is rubbed between the fingers, and a layer of wax adheres to the fingers; gills thick, sub-distant, waxy appearing....... **14**

13. Gills not waxy feeling; gills thin and usually very close together or crowded **15**

14. (13) With hard, brittle, purple gills; on sand .... *Laccaria trullisata* ○

14. With soft, light green to buff gills; on soil .... *Hygrophorus psittacinus* ○

15. (13). Stems shiny white; cap light brown with white scales; spore print purple-brown (Fig. 38) *Hypholoma appendiculata* ☆

15. Stems chalky white, yellow, or brown; spore print not purple-brown... **16**

16. (15) Spore print white............................. **73**

16. Spore print pink *(Entoloma)* **99**

16. Spore print brown.................................**106**

17. (12) Texture of gills waxy when a small bit is crushed between the fingers.: **18**

17. Texture of gills not waxy **19**

18. (17) Gills white, yellow, or orange, widely spaced; spore print white *(Hygrophorus)* . . . . , . . . **78**

18. Gills smoky, close or crowded; spore print black *(Gomphidius)* **171**

19. (17) With white spores (Clitocybe) **76**

19. With pink spores (Clitophilus) **99**

19. With brown spores **124**

20. (9) Annulus or ring present; spore print brown to black **25**

20. Annulus or ring absent; spore print white, pink, or brown to black **21**

21. (20) Gill attachment decurrent; cap broadly convex to plane or occasionally umbilicate (depressed with an umbo in the depression) **22**

21. Gill attachment adnate to adnexed; cap convex to conic or campanulate **24**

22. (21) Spore print white **23**

22. Spore print pink . . . . *Clitopilus prunulus* ☆

23. (22) Growing on leaves, needles, or grass; stem tough; dried specimens revive and regain a fresh appearance when moistened with water; not waxy appearing **87**

23. Growing on wood, among lichens, or in moss; stem fleshy, dried sporocarps do not revive in water; gills waxy appearing **88**

24. (21) Spore print white **89**

24. Spore print brown **132**

24. Spore print purple-brown **156**

24. Spore print black **162**

25. (20) Cap narrowly parabolic to campanulate (bell shaped), covered with fluffy, reddish brown, recurved scales; annulus movable, thin, oblique, often obscure; gills flesh colored turning black with age; spore print black (Fig. 13)
.... *Coprinus comatus* ☆☆☆

25. Cap broadly campanulate, glabrous; annulus membranous and persistent; gills black even in young specimens; spore print black (Fig. 38) .... *Panaeolus separatus* †

25. Cap convex, covered with dense, dark brown hairs; annulus an obscure, hairy ring high on stem; gills light to dark brown, mottled, with white edges; spore print purple-brown to dark brown .... *Psathyrella velutina* ☆

25. Cap mammillate to convex, glabrous; annulus obscure to prominent, often oblique; gills golden to cinnamon brown; spore print cinnamon to rusty brown.............. **131**

26. (1) Spore print brown; stems absent; caps covered with dark brown, small, fibrous scales .... *Crepidotus mollis* ○

26. Spore print white to yellow; stems present or absent; caps glabrous and slightly viscid to dry and covered with scales or squamules.. **28**

gill mushrooms with white, yellowish, greenish, or pale lilac spore print

27. Attachment of cap to stem eccentric or marginal, or margin of cap attached directly to stump or log without a stem.... **28**

27. Attachment of cap to stem central or nearly so **32**

28. (26, 27) Gills hairy, split longitudinally along their edges and rolled back laterally, hence looking like two parallel, radially oriented tubes ...... *Schizophyllum commune* ○

28. Gills not hairy and not split longitudinally along their edges **29**

29. (28) Edge of gills serrate or crenulate; ring present; cap covered with small scales; stem attached almost centrally in some specimens, but almost to margin in others (Fig. 23) .... *Lentinus lepideus* ☆☆

29. Edge of gills smooth; ring absent; cap glabrous or with minute or flattened hairs; stem attachment uniformly near edge of cap, or near center of cap, or stem absent........... **30**

30. (29) Cap tan to dark brown, dry, covered with flattened hairs, round to cordate, flat and depressed at center in maturity, usually attached slightly off center; gills decurrent, mustard yellow to yellow-brown; spore print clay colored to mustard yellow .... *Paxillus atrotomentosus* ☆/✝

30. Cap greenish brown or olive, sticky, fan-shaped to shell-shaped, convex, attached at margin by short stem or plug; gills adnate, pale orange to yellowish tan; spore print yellow.......................... *Pleurotus serotinus* ○

30. Cap white or tan, smooth and moist, attached to stump or log marginally, usually without a stem; gills decurrent, white to cream colored; spore print white to pale lilac or buff **31**

31. (30) Growing on cottonwood, elm, or other hardwoods; cap gray to bluish gray; odor of anise often noticeable; spore print white to buff (Fig. 24)... *Pleurotus ostreatus* ☆☆☆

31. Growing on conifers; caps shiny white; no noticeable odor; spore print white (Fig. 39).... *Pleurotus porrigens* ☆☆☆

32. (27) Base of stem swollen (clavate); volva usually present **33**

32. Base of stem tapered or stem cylindrical, neither tapered at the base nor swollen; volva absent............... **43**

33. (3, 32) Volva a distinct cup; surface of cap smooth or covered by a large patch of veil tissue; gills white to yellow **34**

33. Volva a series of rings, sometimes obscure; surface of cap covered with wart-like patches of tissue; gills white..... **37**

33. Volva indistinct or absent; surface of cap smooth; gills white turning in age to gray or cream colored **38**

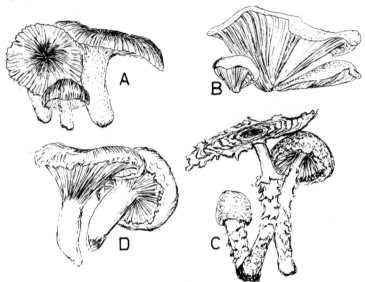

Fig. 39. Some robust, white-spored mushrooms: **A.** *Russula pectinata;* **B.** *Pleurotus porrigens,* the angel wings mushroom; **C.** *Lepiota clypeolaria;* **D.** *Lactarius torminosus,* one of the milky cap mushrooms.

34. (33) Cap yellow to bright orange, large (15 to over 30 cm. in diameter); gills creamy to yellow................. **35**

34. Cap white to pale yellow, medium size (3–15 cm.); gills white **36**

35. (34) Annulus a yellow, skirt-like ring, high on stem; cap bright orange-red; gills yellow   *Amanita caesarea* ○ (☆ ☆ ☆)

35. Annulus thin, often torn loose; cap yellow to orange; gills cream colored ....   *Amanita calyptroderma*   ○ (☆ ☆ ☆)

36. (34) Gills narrow; entire sporocarp white; stems long and slender giving this mushroom an attractive, stately appearance; ring broad, membranous; plant odorless; DO NOT TASTE (Fig. 38)............................   *Amanita virosa* ††

36. Gills broad; caps pale yellowish green; stems short to long; ring skirt-like; odor somewhat resembling raw potatoes but slightly disagreeable; DO NOT TASTE (Fig. 15)
....   *Amanita phalloides* ††

37. (33) Cap gray brown to dingy yellow—sometimes dark cinnamon-brown, in western specimens occasionally white to yellow—with pointed whitish to cream-colored warts; volva fits collar-like at apex of the swollen base (Fig. 18) .... *Amanita pantherina* ☨☨

37. Cap white, yellow to orange, or red, with flat "cottage cheese"-like warts; volva a series of 2–3 relatively obscure rings on or just above the swollen base (Fig. 18) .... *Amanita muscaria* ☨☨○☆

38. (6, 33) Veil usually present and prominent, becoming either a membranous ring which often can slide up and down the stem, or leaving remnants that hang from the margins; gills free from the stem, not waxy **39**

38. Veil present but very fragile, often disappearing entirely; gills adnexed, often becoming free in age, not waxy .... *Amanita baccata* ○[1]

38. Veil absent; gills decurrent; cap and gills very waxy looking and waxy to the touch when crushed .... *Hygrophorus subalpinus* ☆

39. (38) Cap smooth to minutely granular (and hence appearing smooth) **40**

39. Cap covered with scales or squamules **41**

40. (39) Sporocarps small (< 2 cm.) with veil remnants hanging from margin; annulus absent or obscure; caps minutely granular .... *Lepiota seminuda* ○

40. Sporocarps medium sized (4–12 cm.); annulus a white cottony superior ring with a double-fringed edge .... *Lepiota naucina* ○(☆)

1. Do not experiment with any *Amanita*. *A. baccata* might not be poisonous, but it has not been tested; assume that it, and also all edible *Amanitas* you key out, are poisonous. I prefer not to eat either *Amanita* or *Lepiota* species.

41. (39) Gills and spore print green; scales on cap buff to cinnamon; common in lawns and grassland
.... *Chlorophyllum molybdites* †

41. Gills and spore print white to buff; scales on cap reddish brown to reddish gray; found under trees or on compost heaps, etc. **42**

42. (41) Ring collar-like, easily slid up and down the stem, its edge composed of two rows of white hairs; stems long (14–40 cm.), covered with brown scales; cap covered with reddish brown scales; does not change color when bruised
.... *Lepiota procera* ☆ ☆ ☆

42. Ring consisting of fine hairs which disappear at maturity; stems short (3–10 cm.), covered with woolly hairs; cap with brownish scales; flesh soft, white, does not stain (Fig. 39).......................... *Lepiota clypeolaria* †

42. Ring persistent, flaring, with a red-brown, fringed margin; stem medium long (9–15 cm.), hollow near cap, covered with reddish gray squamules; flesh stains orange-yellow fading red-brown when bruised............ *Lepiota rachodes* ☆

43. (32) Milky latex exuded when young stems or caps are broken.. **44**

43. Milky latex not present............................. **53**

44. (8, 43) Latex white, unchanging; cap orange, red, or yellow tinted rose **45**

44. Latex white staining lilac, blue, or yellow; cap buff to brownish gray **49**

44. Latex blood-red to orange; cap carrot colored mixed with green or reddish brown **52**

45. (44) Cap moist to viscid, convex with a depressed center, at least in age **46**

45. Cap dry, convex-knobbed, sometimes depressed in center in age **48**

46. (45) Coloration zoned, orange with bands of reddish orange or yellow with bands of rose; sporocarps relatively large (3–10 cm.); stem light pink or light orange to yellow..... **47**

46. Coloration uniformly maroon red, not zoned; sporocarps small (1.5–5 cm.) stem nearly white near apex to orange-brown near base................. *Lactarius subdulcis* ☆

47. (46) Margin of cap inrolled, cap orange zoned with red-orange; gills adnate to decurrent; found under conifers .... *Lactarius zonarius* ○

47. Margin of cap covered with dense, pinkish, soft hairs, cap yellow tinted rose; gills decurrent; found under paper birch (Fig. 39)......................... *Lactarius torminosus* †

48. (45) Odor sweet, pleasant, clover-like; cap small (1–4 cm.); gills and base of stem brown; found under conifers .... *Lactarius camphoratus* ☆

48. Odor mild, not distinctive; cap medium (2–10 cm.); gills and base of stem white, apex of stem brown; commonly found under hardwoods .... *Lactarius rufus* †

49. (44) Latex white, staining lilac........................ **50**

49. Latex white, staining bluish to greenish gray where wounded........................ *Lactarius mucidus* ○

49. Latex white staining yellow or buff.................. **51**

50. (49) Surface of cap smooth, brownish gray, margin smooth .... *Lactarius uvidus* †

50. Surface of cap pruinose in center, densely woolly near edges, orange-buff; margin fringed with long hairs .... *Lactarius representaneus* †

51. (49) Spore print white; cap light yellowish orange with hairy margin .... *Lactarius scrobiculatus* †

51. Spore print light buff; cap buff to cinnamon .... *Lactarius chrysorheus* †

51. Spore print cinnamon buff; cap orange with red-orange bands........................ *Lactarius sanguifluus* ☆

52. (44) Gills reddish tinged with purple, turning green with age; latex blood-red, scanty; cap uniformly carrot colored .... *Lactarius sanguifluus* ☆

52. Gills bright orange, staining green with age; latex orange, leaving green stains; cap with carrot colored bands alternating with lighter colored bands........ *Lactarius deliciosus* ☆☆

52. Gills whitish; latex blood red, exuded from broken stems; caps red-brown with striate margins.... *Mycena haematopus* ○

53. (43) Stems thick, brittle, often snapping like a piece of chalk.. **54**

53. Stems thick (mostly > 5 mm.) and fleshy fibrous but not brittle.. **63**

53. Stems thin (mostly < 5 mm.) tough, and cartilaginous **85**

54. (9, 53) Caps bright red, purplish red, orange-red, or olivaceous turning red................................. **60**

54. Caps white or dingy, staining brown, yellowish or greenish **55**

55. (54) Gill attachment free or nearly free from stem... **56**

55. Gill attachment adnate to notched.................. **57**

55. Gill attachment decurrent (gills running down the stem) **59**

56. (55) Surface of young sporocarps dry; caps green to grayish green, medium sized (5–12 cm.); stems thin (1–2 cm.) .... *Russula virescens* ○

56. Surface of young sporocarps viscid or sticky; caps yellow, small (2–7 cm.); stems thick (2.5–3 cm.) .... *Russula lutea* ☆

57. (55) Caps olivaceous turning dull green, slightly slimy; gills adnate; flavor mild............ *Russula aeruginea* ☆

57. Caps dark brown in the center, paler brown and conspicuously striate on the margins, viscid; gills adnate to slightly decurrent; flavor peppery (Fig. 39) *Russula pectinata* ☆

57. Caps yellow-orange to yellow-brown, viscid; gills notched; flavor variable....................................... **58**

58. (57) Stems white turning grayish in age and having faint net-like markings on them; gills crowded, light yellow; caps yellow-orange . . . . *Russula ochroleuca* ○

58. Stems white, staining brownish to yellowish in age, not having net-like markings; gills close, broad, often with drops of water on them when young, whitish; caps yellow-brown . . . . *Russula foetans* ○

59. (55) Greenish tinge present on older caps; odor unpleasant, flavor mild; stems short (< 8 cm.—Fig. 25) . . . . *Russula brevipes* ☆☆

59. Greenish tinge not present; odor slight, flavor bitter; stems relatively short (5–12 cm.) . . . . *Russula vesicatoria* ○

60. (54) Having distinct ridges on the stems; odor slightly fishy; caps orange-red . . . . *Russula paludosa* ☆

60. Having smooth stems; odor mild; caps not orange-red. . . **61**

61. (60) Sporocarps large (mostly 10–35 cm.); flavor mild . . . **62**

61. Sporocarps small (4–12 cm.); flavor peppery (Fig. 25) . . . . *Russula emetica* †

62. (61) Caps purple-red; stems white tinged with red . . . . *Russula alutacea* ☆☆

62. Caps olive turning red with age; stems thick with rosy tinge. . . . . *Russula olivacea* ☆

63. (53) Odor fishy or skunk-like; cap flat, slimy, orange . . . . *Hygrophorus laetus* ○

63. Odor not fishy or skunk-like; cap otherwise. **64**

64. (63) Gills free from stem or nearly so. **65**

64. Gills attached to stem **67**

65. (64) Cap conic to a narrow peak, orange-red, viscid, relatively small (2–9 cm.); gills yellowish, bruising black, waxy feeling when crushed between the fingers (Fig. 38) . . . . *Hygrophorus conicus* ○

65. Cap broadly convex to plane, white to yellow, dry to slightly viscid, relatively large (5–20 cm.) covered with brown scales; gills white to pink, sometimes bruising pink; not waxy feeling
.... **66**

66. (11, 65) With bright yellow cap and thick, scaly white stem .... *Armillaria albolanaripes* ○
66. With white cap sometimes tinged pale yellow, and tapering stem, reddish below and white above the skirt-like ring
.... *Armillaria ponderosa* ☆☆

67. (64) Growing in clumps of 3 to 30 or more in tall grass, often hidden; caps creamy to tan, smooth, persistently rounded; stems flattened and/or curved; odor pleasant........ **68**
67. Growing singly or in small clumps, usually not hidden in tall grass; caps and stems otherwise..................... **69**

68. (67) Spores smooth, rounded, white; caps soapy feeling when moist; clumps large, 5 to 30 or more
.... *Lyophyllum multiceps* ☆☆
68. Spores angular, reddish, but often so pale as to appear white; caps not soapy feeling; clumps mostly 2 to 5 (Fig. 16)
.... *Entoloma sinuatum* ††

69. (67) Attachment of gills to stem adnate (square) to adnexed (notched) **70**
69. Attachment of gills to stem decurrent (extending down the stem) **76**

70. (69) Ring present..................................... **71**
70. Ring absent **73**

71. (70) Cap honey yellow to pinkish brown or brown; growing in clusters of a few to many on wood, often on a living tree
.... *Armillaria mellea* ☆☆☆
71. Cap orange-brown to rusty; growing singly or in groups under conifers...................................... **72**

72. (71) Annulus dingy white to rusty, hanging down (Fig. 40) .... *Cystoderma fallax* ○
72. Annulus white, flaring upward .... *Armillaria zelleri* ○
72. Annulus pinkish, very thin to obscure .... *Hygrophorus subalpinus* ☆

73. (16, 70) Color of caps a rich grass-green, caps conic to convex or campanulate, glutinous to viscid; stems slimy viscid, green .... *Hygrophorus psittacinus* ○
73. Color of the caps white, caps plane, dry smooth; stems dry, hairy, whitish.................... *Clitocybe irina* ☆☆☆
73. Color of the caps dingy brown to reddish brown, caps convex, dry to tacky, covered with small scales, flattened hairs, or grains of sand; stems chalky white to reddish brown **74**

74. (73) Growing in sand or on sand dunes; gills purple, waxy; stems curved or twisted; caps moist to tacky .... *Laccaria trullisata* ○
74. Growing in soil under conifers; gills white, not waxy; stems straight; caps dry................................... **75**

75. (74) Margin of caps incurved, caps grayish brown; stems chalky white (Fig. 40) .... *Tricholoma pardin* †
75. Margin of caps hairy; caps reddish brown; stems reddish brown with white zone at apex... *Tricholoma vaccinum* ○

76. (19, 69) Caps white, mostly moist to viscid.......... **77**
76. Caps olive brown to buff or orange, mostly dry...... **80**

77. (76) Gills waxy feeling; caps convex to flat, moist to viscid **78**
77. Gills not waxy; caps depressed, dry.... *Clitocybe dealbata* †

78. (18, 77) Sporocarps small (1–4 cm.); caps moist, not viscid, with slightly striate margins in age *Hygrophorus borealis* ○
78. Sporocarps medium sized (2–10 cm.) caps viscid to glutinous **79**

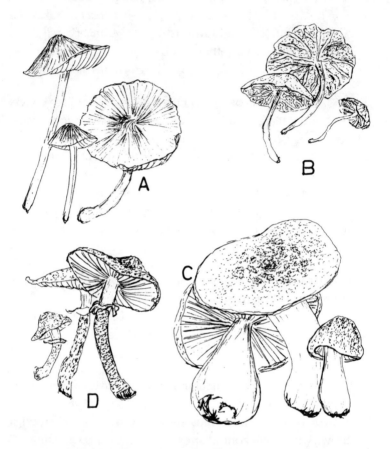

Fig. 40. Some delicate white-spored mushrooms: **A.** *Marasmius oreades,* the fairy ring mushroom; **B.** *Marasmius magnisporus;* **C.** *Tricholoma pardin;* **D.** *Cystoderma fallax.*

78. Sporocarps large (5–25 cm.); caps viscid; gills very waxy
    .... *Hygrophorus subalpinus* ☆

79. (78) Surface of caps covered with minute, yellow hairs
    giving it a yellowish appearance; stems white with yellow
    apex.......................... *Hygrophorus chrysodon* ☆
79. Surface of caps smooth, without hairs; stems white hollow
    .... *Hygrophorus eberneus* ☆

80. (76) Gills plate-like with distinctly serrate to crenulate margins; mature caps convex to convex-knobbed, covered with many brown-tipped scales...... *Lentinus tigrinis* ○

80. Gills plate-like with entire or nearly entire margins; mature caps flat to depressed, smooth to pubescent **81**

80. Gills blunt to vein-like; caps depressed to funnel-shaped, smooth or covered with flattened yellowish scales... **83**

81. (80) Caps viscid when wet, olive brown; gills buff; stems long (12–18 cm.), pinkish buff... *Armillaria imperialis* ○

81. Caps dry to moist, not viscid when wet, pinkish or orange-brown; stems short (2–10 cm.) pinkish brown to orange **82**

82. (81) Having bright orange, narrow, forked gills and orange stem; caps convex or flat to depressed, brownish orange .... *Clitocybe aurantiaca* †

82. Having flesh-colored to pinkish, thick, well separated gills and pinkish brown stem and cap; caps convex or flat .... *Laccaria laccata* ☆

83. (80) Color of caps and gills orange **84**

83. Color of caps and gills white   *Cantharellus subalbidus* ☆☆☆

84. (83) Caps smooth, depressed in center with an umbo or knob usually in the center of the depression; sporocarps luminescent after 2–4 minutes in the dark or after holding at room temperature wrapped in wax paper for 2–3 hours .... *Clitocybe illudens* †

84. Caps smooth, depressed in center but lacking an umbo; sporocarps not luminescent ... *Cantharellus cibarius* ☆☆☆

84. Caps covered with erect scales, depressed in center but lacking an umbo; sporocarps not luminescent ....*Cantharellus floccosus* †

85. (53) Gills decurrent; caps broadly convex to plane or depressed... **86**

85. Gills adnate to adnexed; caps convex to conic or campanulate **89**

86. (85) Growing on leaves, needles, or grass; stem tough; gills not waxy................................... **87**

86. Growing on wood among lichens or moss; stem fleshy; gills waxy.................................... **88**

87. (23, 86) With gills very widely spaced; cap convex; found on raspberry canes and dead hardwood stems (Fig. 40) .... *Marasmius magnisporus* ○

87. With gills relatively closely spaced; cap umbilicate or sometimes mammillate with pronounced nipple; found mostly in coniferous forests ... *Marasmius umbilicatus* ○

88. (23, 86) Immature caps convex becoming depressed in age, straw colored.................. *Omphalina ericetorum* ○

88. Immature caps depressed, yellow   *Omphalina wynniae* ○

89. (24, 85) Broken stems exuding a blood red latex; caps red-brown with striate margin; found singly or in clusters on wood....................... *Mycena haematopus* ○

89. Broken stems not exuding latex; caps variable **90**

90. (89) Growng in dense clusters on wood; stems 4–10 cm. long, united at base; caps reddish brown, dry, striate .... *Collybia acervata* ☆☆

90. Growing singly or in small groups; stems and caps otherwise **91**

91. (90) Stems white with tint of yellow or gray, growing on logs, litter, or deep humus............................... **92**

91. Stems reddish brown, at least at base; growing in lawns or on conifer logs **93**

91. Stems shiny black; growing on conifer needles .... *Marasmius androsaceus* ○

92. (91) Growing in deep humus or leaf litter; stems white with tint of yellow.........................*Collybia dryophila* †

92. Growing on decaying hardwood logs or stumps; stems grayish white, glabrous............. *Mycena galericula* ☆

93. (91) The stems pinkish brown covered with white hairs at the base; growing on conifer logs and stumps
.... *Mycena overholzii* ○

93. The stems buff at apex, lighter than caps, reddish brown at base; growing in circles (fairy rings) in lawns and meadows (Fig. 40)...................... *Marasmius oreades* ☆☆☆

gill mushrooms with pink, salmon, or flesh-brown spore print

94. Gills free from stem, the cap breaking readily from the stem... **95**

94. Gills adnexed, adnate, or decurrent, clinging to the stem when cap is broken away, or leaving a small piece of gill on the stem.. **99**

95. (94) Having a volva but no ring; caps white or dingy yellow
.... **96**

95. Having neither volva nor ring; caps dark yellow to brown
.... **97**

96. (95) Sporocarps small (1–3 cm.) white; growing on other mushrooms (Fig. 41)............. *Volvariella surrecta* ○

96. Sporocarps large (5–20 cm.), dingy yellow; on wood
.... *Volvariella bombycina* ○

97. (7, 95) Caps dark yellow, sometimes olive yellow, convex to campanulate, with umbo.......... *Pluteus admirabilis* ○

97. Caps dark brown, flat to convex or campanulate, lacking umbo... **98**

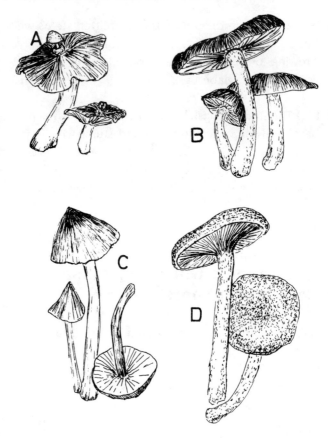

Fig. 41. Some pink-spored mushrooms: **A.** *Volvariella surrecta* growing on *Clitocybe nebularis;* **B.** *Pluteus cervinus;* **C.** *Entoloma salmoneum;* **D.** *Clitopilus prunulus.*

98. (97) Gills having a dark edge (need a magnifying glass to see this) . . . . *Pluteus umbrinus* ☆☆
98. Gills lacking a dark edge (Fig. 41) . . . . *Pluteus cervinus* ☆☆

99. (16, 19, 24, 94) Odor of fresh sporocarps pleasantly farinaceous, like newly milled wheat; caps mostly campanulate to convex; mostly solitary **100**
99. Odor of sporocarps similar to that of burnt sugar; caps conical; growing in clumps of 2–5 in tall grass (Fig. 16) . . . . *Entoloma sinuatum* ††

100. (99) Spores (10–12 x 5–7 μ*) longitudinaly striate; cap grayish, dry, unpolished, convex becoming flat; gills close with vinaceous tints (Fig. 41) ...... *Clitopilus prunulus* ☆

100. Spores (< 10 μ max diam.) angular; cap tan to brown, bell-shaped becoming convex **101**

100. Spores (10–13 x 10–13 μ) angular; caps orange to salmon-pink, conical (Fig. 41) .... *Entoloma salmoneum* ○

101. (100) Stem often twisted or flattened, about as long as cap diameter; spores egg-shaped, angular, and warted; gills close .... *Entoloma sericeum* ○ (☆)

101. Stems straight and cylindrical, longer than cap diameter; spores angular but nearly round, gills fairly well separated (Fig. 16) .... *Entoloma lividum* ††

gill mushrooms with brown, yellowish brown, clay brown, or cinnamon spore print

102. Caps attached centrally to the stems **103**

102. Caps eccentric, or attached at the margin without stems **140**

103. (102) Stems thick (mostly > 5 mm.), fleshy fibrous **104**

103. Stems thin (mostly < 5 mm.), tough, cartilaginous, and stringy **128**

104. (103) Having neither a distinct annulus nor a volva; however, faint markings may be present on the stem indicating where the inner veil broke away from the stem **105**

104. Having an annulus but usually not a volva......... **125**

* Spores are measured in micrometers (abbrev. μ). There are 10,000 μ to 1 centimeter.

105. (7, 104) Gills free from the stem in both young and old specimens....................... *Pluteolus callisteus* ○
105. Gills adnate to adnexed, sometimes becoming free in age **106**
105. Gills decurrent.................................... **124**

106. (16, 105) Caps bluish lavender, lilac, or bluish green **107**
106. Caps mostly some shade of yellow or brown, not bluish or lilac.. **108**

107. (106) With bright bluish lavender caps; stems white with a bluish lavender sheath; caps sticky when wet .... *Cortinarius subfoetidus* ○
107. With lilac colored caps and stems, and dry, fibrillose caps (Fig. 42)......................... *Cortinarius traganus* ○

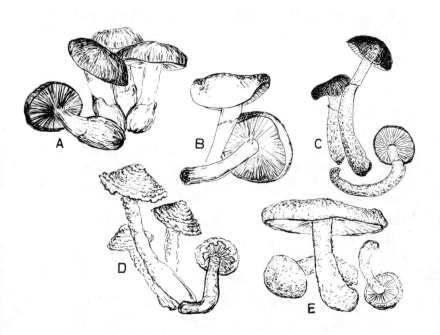

Fig. 42. Examples of robust mushrooms with brown spores: **A.** *Cortinarius traganus;* **B.** *Gymnopilus terrestris;* **C.** *Pholiota squarrosoides;* **D.** *Pholiota squarrosa;* **E.** *Hebeloma sinapizans* or "poison pie."

107. With bluish green, slimy, sticky cap, and white to greenish stem . . . . *Pholiota subcaerulea* ○

108. (106) Stems very short, about half as long to as long as the cap diameter; sporocarps subterranean; cortina bluish gray and persisting to maturity . . . *Cortinarius bigelowii* ○
108. Stems relatively long, at least as long as the cap diameter; sporocarps above ground; cortina, if present, brown, yellow, or white, and present only in the young sporocarps **109**

109. (108) Scales or scale-like veil remnants present on both caps and stems. **110**
109. Scales or scale-like veil remnants present on stems but not on caps. **113**
109. Scales or scale-like veil remnants present on neither stems nor caps, or present on caps only. **116**

110. (109) The scales pointed and numerous on both caps and stems. **111**
110. The scales broad to spot-like, gelatinous or fibrillose, and scattered. **112**

111. (110) Caps dry; odor when flesh is broken or crushed onion-like; spores small (3.5–4.5 x 5–8 mu) and lacking an apical pore (Fig. 42). . . . . *Pholiota squarrosa* †
111. Caps viscid under the scales; no onion-like odor; spores very small (2.5–3.5 x 4–6 mu) with an apical pore (Fig. 42)
. . . . *Pholiota squarrosoides* ☆☆☆

112. (110) With broad, gelatinous scales on both cap and stem
. . . . *Pholiota hiemale* †
112. With spot-like gelatinous scales on the cap and dry, tawny scales low on the stem. . . . . *Pholiota aurivella* ○(☆)
112. With small, scattered scales on the cap, and pointed scales on the stem. *Pholiota terrestris* ○(☆)

113. (109) Gills pallid, considerably lighter in color than the cap and stem; scales on stem membranous, rather obscure remnants of the inner veil. **114**

113. Gills tan to brown, about the same color as the cap and stem; scales on stem distinct though sometimes small   **115**

114. (113) A cortina, or cobweb-like veil, present on the young sporocarps; caps smooth, tawny, medium-sized (4–6 cm.); slime sheath on stems separating into light and dark patches of yellow...................... *Cortinarius palludifolius* ○
114. A cortina, or veil, not present at any time; caps small (1–3 cm.) with appressed scales near the margin; stems with zones of reddish coloration .... *Pholiota fulvozonata* ○

115. (113) Caps glabrous, convex, with light colored aurea at apex, small (1–3 cm.); ring-like zone high on stem, stem glabrous above this zone, covered with small scales below; growing on wood, often on buried wood
.... *Pholiota mutabilis* ○ (☆☆)
115. Caps rough, convex to plane, uniformly colored, medium to large (6–13 cm.); entire stem covered with small, distinct scales; mycorrhizal or growing on leaf litter or duff, not on wood (Fig. 42) .... *Hebeloma sinapizans* ○

116. (109) Surface of cap having broad, spot-like, gelatinous scales; stems slightly rough but not scaly *Pholiota abietis* ○
116. Surface of cap as well as stems lacking scales **117**

117. (116) Caps striate from the presence of dull brown, radially appressed fibrils; growing on slash... *Pholiota decorata* ○
117. Caps mostly glabrous, not striate from radially appressed fibrils; growing on wood, soil, or moss.............. **118**

118. (117) Spore deposit yellow-brown to brown; caps dingy white to grayish tan, plane to slightly depressed; stems dull white to yellowish tan, cylindrical or sometimes bulbous at base; odor like radishes; droplets of water often on gills
................................*Hebeloma crustuliniforme* †
118. Spore deposit bright rusty-brown; caps bright orange-brown, glabrous, plane to slightly convex; stems bright tan to cinnamon, slightly clavate; odor mild; no droplets of water on gills (Fig. 42) .... *Gymnopilis terrestris* ○

118. Spore deposit dull rusty-brown to earth brown; caps mostly tan to dull brown, conic to convex, sometimes almost flat; stems white to dark brown with dull tones prevailing, either tapered, cylidrical, or decidedly clavate............. **119**

119. (118) Stems clavate to bulbous, tapering to a thickened base or abruptly swollen at the base; cobweb-like cortina usually present in young sporocarps................ **120**
119. Stems cylindrical to tapered, base equal to or smaller than the apex of the stem; cobweb-like cortina usually not present **121**

120. (119) Cortina and stem yellow, slimy; stem short with fibrillose patches; odor of freshly husked corn .... *Cortinarius superbus* ○
120. Cortina and stem brown, dry; stem fairly long with red bands encircling it; odor of radishes.... *Cortinarius armillatus* ☆

121. (119) Caps small (1–3 cm.), pale yellow, sticky; young gills yellow; stem becoming rusty from base up; growing in clumps of 5 to 10 or more ...... *Pholiota subochracea* ○
121. Caps small to large, orange-brown to brown, dry to viscid; young gills white to pallid; in clumps or solitary **122**

122. (121) Sporocarps large (4–12 cm.) with cobweb-like veil when young.................. *Cortinarius subaustralis* ○
122. Sporocarps small (1–5 cm.) and lacking a cobweb-like veil **123**

123. (122) With dense hairs on a dark brown conic to convex cap .... *Inocybe lanuginosa* ☆
123. Without dense hairs on a brownish orange to red-orange, convex to flat cap................ *Pholiota sublubrica* ○

124. (19, 105) Flesh bruising blue to brown; caps small to medium sized (2–6 cm.), convex, often cracked; gills lemon yellow......................... *Pholiota rhodoxanthus* ☆

124. Flesh bruising brown but not blue; caps large (4–12 cm.) convex to plane, depressed in center at maturity, covered with matted soft hair; gills yellowish olive
.... *Paxillus involutus* ○

125. (11, 104) Sporocarps small to medium (1–10 cm.), orange to brown... **126**
125. Sporocarps large (5–30 cm.), whitish to yellow..... **127**

126. (125) Ring hairy; cap viscid, brown   *Hebeloma mesophaeum* †
126. Ring membranous; cap dry, orange, with a persistent white veil....................... *Rozites caperata* ☆☆☆

127. (125) Color a striking golden yellow; caps sometimes very large (5–20, occasionally 30 cm.), dry   *Pholiota aurea* ○(☆)
127. Color off-white; caps large (5–20 cm.), viscid, minutely scaly............................... *Pholiota destruens* ☆

128. (103) Gills decurrent............................. **129**
128. Gills adnate to adnexed, sometimes appearing to be free
.... **130**

129. (128) Caps translucent when wet, appearing striate because the gills show through.............. *Tubaria pellucida* ○
129. Caps not translucent, covered with scurfy, dandruff-like scales............................. *Tubaria furfuracea* ○

130. (128) Annulus present; caps, stems, gills cinnamon to bay brown **131**
130. Annulus absent; caps, stems, gills variable in color.... **132**

131. (25, 130) Ring rather obscure, oblique; apex of cap rounded; growing in lawns (Fig. 17)........... *Galerina venenata* ††
131. Ring prominent, membranous, at right angles to stem; apex of cap a prominent nipple; growing in moss (Fig. 43)
.... *Galerina paludosa* ○

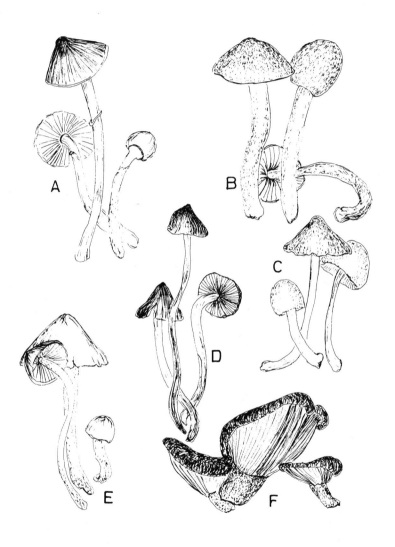

Fig. 43. Examples of LBM's or delicate brown-spored mushrooms:
A. *Galerina paludosa;*   **B.** *Inocybe olympiana;*   **C.** *Bolbitius vitellinus;*
D. *Phaeocollybia fallax;*   **E.** *Agrocybe acericola;*   **F.** *Paxillus atrotomentosus.*

131. Ring prominent, hairy, at right angles to stem; apex of cap a low knob; growing on wood (Fig. 17)
.... *Galerina autumnalis* ††

132. (24, 130) The color of the caps distinctly brown, usually cinnamon brown to ocherous brown **133**
132. The color of the caps white to yellow or lilac **138**

133. (132) Caps plane to convex, or campanulate when young, but not mammillate; umbo lacking (Fig. 43)
.... *Agrocybe acericola* ○ (☆)
133. Caps mammillate with a prominent umbo, or nipple, at the apex of most of the caps......................... **134**
133. Caps narrowly conic to campanulate but not mammillate; umbo lacking **135**

134. (133) Nipple very broad, flat; caps ocherous brown, 1.5–3 cm. broad; young gills reddish brown; growing on soil in coniferous forests (Fig. 43)........... *Inocybe olympiana* ○
134. Nipple rounded, prominent, caps tawny ocherous, 0.5–2 cm. broad, young gills reddish brown; growing on moss in bogs (Fig. 43) .... *Galerina palludosa* ○[1]
134. Nipple pointed or conic; caps glabrous, slimy, olivaceous brown, 0.5–1.5 cm. broad; young gills dull lilac; growing on wet soil in spruce forests (Fig. 43)
.... *Phaeocollybia fallax* ○

135. (133) Annulus present on young sporocarps but often disappears; caps broad parabolic to campanulate or occasionally convex, cinnamon to ocherous brown.... **136**
135. Annulus absent on young as well as old sporocarps; caps narrowly or sharply conic, yellowish brown to dark reddish-brown **137**

136. (135) Growing on moss; sporocarps small (0.5–2 cm.), dry .... *Galerina cerina* ◯[1]

136. Growing on wood or sometimes in lawns or meadows; sporocarps medium sized (2–5 cm.), viscid (Fig. 17) .... *Galerina autumnalis* ††

137. (135) The sporocarps are very small (0.5–2 cm.) with bright yellow-brown spores having a pore at the apex; gills free; caps yellowish brown to dark reddish brown .... *Conocybe tenera* ◯

137. The sporocarps are medium-sized (2–6 cm.) with rusty brown spores lacking a pore at the apex; gills notched; caps yellowish brown..................... *Inocybe fastigiata* †

138. (132) A pore present at the apex of each bright yellow-brown spore; young caps cream colored to bright yellow, convex to conic, but not mammilate, viscid......... **139**

138. A pore not present on the rusty brown spores; young and old caps white to violet, mammilate with a very small umbo or nipple, dry....................... *Inocybe geophylla* †

139. (138) Mature caps convex to bell shaped, yellowish brown; young caps bright yellow (Fig. 43)..... *Bolbitius vitellinus* ◯

139. Mature caps conic to bell-shaped, cream colored; young caps cream colored............. *Agrocybe pediades* ◯ (☆)

140. (102) Stem absent, cap attached to stump or log by its margin; spores smooth, yellowish brown; sporocarp covered with dense small scales .... *Crepidotus mollis* ◯

140. Stem attachment eccentric; spores smooth, mustard yellow to clay colored; sporocarps covered with matted soft hairs (Fig. 43) .... *Paxillus atrotomentosus* ☆ /†

1. **All** *Galerinas* are under suspicion. Most species that have been tested contain powerful toxins. DO NOT EXPERIMENT with any of them.

gill mushrooms with purple-brown to chocolate-brown spore print

141. Gills free, stem easily removable from cap, breaking away clean **142**

141. Gills attached, stems not easily removable from caps **147**

142. (6, 141) Caps white at first, sometimes turning tan or brownish **143**

142. Caps yellow-brown to reddish brown............. **145**

143. (142) Annulus or ring single or lacking (Fig. 29)
.... *Agaricus campestris* ☆☆☆

143. Annulus or ring double........................... **144**

144. (143) Flesh staining yellow when bruised
.... *Agaricus arvensis* ○ (☆☆)

144. Flesh not staining when bruised but turning yellow when a drop of KOH is applied to a cut surface
.... *Agaricus silvicola* ○ (☆☆)

145. (142) Caps yellow brown, very large (10–25 cm., occasionally 40 cm.) sporocarps have the odor of onions
.... *Agaricus augustus* ☆☆☆

145. Caps reddish brown, medium sized (4–12 cm.); no odor of onions **146**

146. (145) With firm, white flesh which slowly turns reddish brown when bruised .... *Agaricus silvaticus* ☆

146. With firm, white flesh which slowly turns yellow when bruised............................ *Agaricus hondensis* †

147. (141) Annulus present, membranous and persistent... **148**

147. Annulus, if present, a thin zone of fibrils which does not persist **152**

148. (11, 147) Stem covered with scales; caps relatively large (2–14 cm.) **149**

148. Stems not scaly; caps small (1–cm.) **151**

149. (148) Scales large, rough, on cap and stem below ring
.... *Stropharia kaufmanii* ○
149. Scales cottony **150**

150. (149) Ring usually disappearing at maturity; stems scaly but cap not scaly.................. *Stropharia ambigua* ☆
150. Ring persistent; both cap and stems scaly
.... *Stropharia hornemanni* ○

151. (148) Cap bright green (Fig. 44)
.... *Stropharia aeruginosa* ☆/†○
151. Cap yellow-brown (Fig. 44)....... *Stropharia coronilla* ☆

152. (147) Stems thick (mostly > 5 mm.), more or less fleshy fibrous... **153**
152. Stems thin (mostly 2–4 mm.) stringy, tough, and cartilaginous **156**

153. (152) Growing in large cespitose clusters on wood; caps orange to yellow................................... **154**
153. Growing singly or in groups in grassy areas or under conifers; caps cinnamon to dark brown..................... **155**

154. (153) Gills white becoming gray or purple-brown but not greenish .... *Naematoloma capnoides* ☆☆
154. Gills sulfur yellow with a greenish hue
.... *Naematoloma fasciculare* †

155. (153) Spores smooth; caps relatively large (2–14 cm.), cinnamon to purplish brown with white cottony scales; growing under conifers .... *Stropharia ambigua* ☆
155. Spores warty; caps small (1–5 cm.), dark brown, not scaly; growing in lawns or grassy areas... *Psathyrella velutina* ☆

156. (24, 152) Caps flat to convex **157**
156. Caps conic to campanulate....................... **158**

157. (156) Growing in cespitose clumps on hardwood; caps viscid, colored in zones; margins white, apex pale tan (Fig. 44) .... *Psathyrella hydrophylla* ○
157. Growing in lawns or grassy areas in groups, not cespitose; caps dry, pale brown to white, not zoned (Fig. 38) .... *Hypholoma appendiculatum* ☆

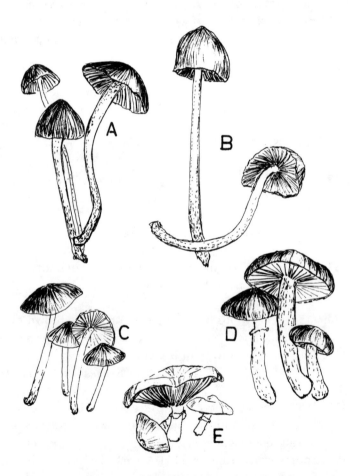

Fig. 44. Examples of mushrooms with purplish brown or smoky brown spore print: **A.** *Panaeolus foenisecii*, **B.** *Naematoloma dispersum*, **C.** *Psathyrella hydrophila*, **D.** *Stropharia aeruginosa*, **E.** *Stropharia coronilla*.

158. (156) Gills close, cinnamon to purple-brown with white edges; on wood debris, moss, or in grassy areas......**159**
158. Gills separated, gray brown to chocolate brown without white on the edges; on dung..... *Psilocybe coprophila* ○

159. (158) Sporocarps dry or moist to the touch, not viscid **160**
159. Sporocarps viscid (sticky or slippery but not slimy) .... *Psilocybe coerulipes* ○

160. (159) Growing on moss; caps moist, dark red-brown .... *Psilocybe montana* ○
160. Growing on wood debris; caps dry, orange-brown (Fig. 44) .... *Naematoloma dispersum* ○
160. Growing in lawns or grassy areas; caps dry, smoky brown to reddish brown (Fig. 44) .... *Panaeolus foenisecii* ☆

gill mushrooms with smoky gray to black spore print

161. Gills free, adnexed, or adnate, not extending down the stem; caps conic to campanulate; spore print black.... **162**
161. Gills decurrent, extending down the stem; caps convex to flat, often depressed in center or with upturned margins; spore print smoky gray........................... **171**

162. (24, 161) Sporocarps very small and delicate, caps 0.5–1.5 cm. broad; stems 1–2 mm. thick; caps deeply striate, often folded umbrella-like; gills well separated; abundant on well decayed wood or grass...................... **163**
162. Sporocarps small to large, 1–8 cm. broad; stems mostly 3–10 mm. thick; caps not striate except at margins, nor folded umbrella-like; gills close to crowded; growing on dung, wood debris, rotten logs, grass, or hard ground **164**

163. (162) Growing in large troops on wood debris; gills adnate, do not deliquesce in age (Fig. 45)
.... *Coprinus disseminatus* ○
163. Growing in groups in grass; gills free but attached to a collar, deliquesce slowly in age............ *Coprinus plicatilis* ○

164. (162) Young gills white to gray, turning black and finally deliquescing in age, adnexed or notched to nearly free; annulus, if present, either high or low on stem, not midway; growing on wood debris, in grass, or in hard ground, parking lots, etc., rarely on dung **165**
164. Young gills mottled blackish-brown or black, never deliquescing in age, adnate; annulus, if present, midway on stems; growing on horse or cow dung.............. **169**

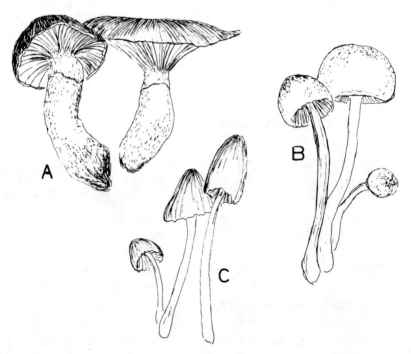

Fig. 45. Some mushrooms with black spores: **A.** *Gomphidius glutinosa*, **B.** *Panaeolus campanulatus*, **C.** *Coprinus disseminatus*, **D.** *Chroogomphus tomentosus*.

165. (11, 164) Caps small (1–2 cm.), narrowly conic when young, pure white; annulus high on stem, hairy
.... *Coprinus niveus* ○

165. Caps large (2–8 cm.), parabolic to campanulate, gray brown or white with reddish scales; annulus, if present, low **166**

166. (165) Mature caps, prior to deliquescing, tall and cylindrical, covered with numerous flattened, reddish scales which curve upward; not striate (Fig. 13)
.... *Coprinus comatus*☆ ☆ ☆

166. Mature caps, prior to deliquescing, conic to bell-shaped, with or without small scales at apex only; caps often striate.. **167**

167. (166) Glistening white particles present on the center of young caps, disappearing in age; caps reddish brown; stems white without a colored zone at its base; spore print blackish brown; growing on wood debris or around stumps, seldom in grass.................... *Coprinus micaceus* ☆

167. Glistening white particles not present on the caps; caps gray to grayish brown; stems usually white above with a colored zone at base; spore print black; growing in grass or at the base of living trees **168**

168. (167) Occurring singly or, more often, in large, cespitose clumps at base of elm, willow, or cottonwood trees or in grass; stems white with olive-brown base; spores smooth; common in North America (and Europe)
.... *Coprinus atramentarius* ☆☆

168. Occurring singly or in small clumps at base of maple or other hardwood trees; stems white without colored zone at base; spores rough; rare in North America (common in Europe) .... *Coprinus insignis* †

169. (164) Annulus present and persistent; cap viscid (Fig. 38)
.....................................*Panaeolus separatus* †

169. Annulus not present; cap dry...................... **170**

170. (169) Center of cap wrinkled; caps small (0.7–3.5 cm.)
....*Panaeolus retirugis* †
170. Center of cap not wrinkled; cap small to medium-sized
(0.8–5 cm.–Fig. 45).............. *Panaeolus campanulatus* †

171. (18, 161) Flesh light orange to salmon; cap dry to viscid
.... **172**
171. Flesh white; cap glutinous (slimy) **173**

172. (171) Color orange to grayish buff; cap dry (Fig. 45)
.... *Chroogomphus tomentosus* ☆
172. Color reddish brown; cap more or less viscid
.... *Chroogomphus rutilus* ☆

173. (171) Veil present, leaving a ring high on the stem which
becomes black as the spores are discharged........ **174**
173. Veil absent, ring absent........ *Gomphidius maculatis* ☆

174. (173) Growing in cespitose clusters; caps a dingy salmon
color; base of stems buried in the soil
.... *Gomphidus oregonensis* ☆
174. Growing solitary or in scattered groups; caps red to purplish;
base of stem yellow, not buried.................... **175**

175. (174) Flesh thick, firm, white; caps red; young gills white
.... *Gomphidius subroseus* ☆☆
175. Flesh thick, soft, white; caps purple-brown; gills drab
gray (Fig. 45) .... *Gomphidius glutinosus* ☆

mushroom families & genera

Whenever a new species of fungus is discovered, a detailed description of it is published in a scientific journal or book. It is then assigned to genus and family and given a species name consisting of two parts, the name of the genus to which it has been assigned and a species epithet that has never before been used for any member of that genus. Whenever we are in doubt as to the identity of a mushroom, we may compare it with the original description of that species to confirm our identification. Unfortunately, the species descriptions are often difficult to locate; however, excellent genus descriptions are found in many books on mushrooms along with detailed descriptions and color photographs of some of the species. Before eating any mushroom identified through the keys in Chapter Five, make careful comparisons to the genus descriptions in this chapter and then compare it with pictures and detailed species descriptions form several sources. Adequate descriptions of the Foolproof Four and eleven other groups of edible mushrooms are given in Chapters Two and Four, but as you go on to more difficult groups of mushrooms, you will need to be increasingly critical in order to avoid being poisoned.

The more than ninety genera of mushrooms found in the keys in Chapter Five and/or referred to elsewhere in this book, along with the mushroom families and orders to which they belong, are briefly described in this chapter. Before you read these descriptions, you may want to review the descriptive terms in Chapter One.

classification of mushrooms. Some mycologists are "lumpers," others are "splitters." Consequently, many different classification systems exist for the fungi. For example, what I have called *Ramaria pyxidata* in this book is described as *Clavaria pyxidata* in many books and as *Clavicorona pyxidata* in others. Where a large, unwieldly

genus (like the traditional *Clavaria*) is made up of groups of species which consistently differ from each other in several significant ways, I have followed the "splitters" and recognized the new names that have appeared in recent years. Where the species included in two or more genera form a continuum of populations having overlapping characterisitics, I have usually followed the "lumpers" and stayed with the older genus name.

To help those who use other books in conjunction with this one, I have indicated, in parentheses, at the end of each genus description, some of the segregate genera (abbreviated *seg.*) that "splitters" have created in recent years. The international rules of botanical nomenclature specify that whenever a species is transferred from one genus to another, as the result of either splitting or lumping, or for other reasons, the species epithet must not be changed unless there is already another species in the new genus with the same species epithet. Knowing the names of segregate genera, and knowing that the species epithet will be the same in the segregate genus as it is in this book, can help you find pictures and descriptions of mushrooms in books using different names than I have used.

The international rules of botanical nomenclature also specify that names of plant families must end with the suffix *-aceae* and plant orders with the suffix *-ales.* Genus names, on the other hand, are Latin or Latinized nouns and have no consistent ending. Following each genus name in the following list, the family to which it belongs is indicated by the first four letters of the family name in capital letters. Immediately after the family designation, the total number of known species in that genus is indicated, followed by another number indicating how many of the species are included in the keys in this book. Where a recent monograph of North American species has been published, this is also indicated with the letters *NA* following the number. The *NA* figures will invariably be more accurate than the worldwide figures for several reasons: More recent data, inclusion of recently discovered species, and elimination of synonyms. The distinguishing characteristics of the genus are then given in enough detail so that the genus can be positively identified. If you have keyed a mushroom to species but are not fully satisfied that your identification is correct, carefully compare your specimen with the genus description. If they match, you can then consult a specialized monograph for that species for positive identification, likely to a species not included in this book. For each genus, only a small percentage of the species can be keyed with the aid of this book. Even though I have tried to include all the **common** mushrooms of North America in the keys, along with many other species, you are certain to find one of the thousands of species not included sooner or later. However, the genus to which it belongs will almost certainly be in the key, as well as the family. For example, Table 1 in Chapter Five, at the beginning of Key F (page 132) can be consulted to decide the possible genera that an unknown gill mushroom could belong to.

Mushrooms belong to two of the 30 or so classes of plants, the Ascomyceteae and the Basidiomyceteae. Each class is divided into several orders. Two orders of Ascomyceteae, the Pezizales and the Tuberales, include species that produce fleshy sporocarps that are often eaten; while three orders of Basidiomyceteae contain most of the mushrooms: the Aphyllophorales, Agaricales, and Lycoperdales. Six additional orders contain fleshy fungi resembling mushrooms, a few of which are edible: The Tremellales, Auriculariales, Hymenogastrales, Podaxales, Phallales, and Nidulariales. Each of these eleven orders is divided into families. The fleshy fungi we eat belong to about 28 families.

Most mushrooms belong to the Agaricales, a large order containing 15 families and probably 6000 or more species. Most Agaricales produce their spores on the surface of thin, flat, vertical plates called gills. Spores are produced in vertical tubes in a few species of Agaricales. For convenience, the Agaricales is divided into three suborders, the Agaricineae with 11 families, the Boletineae with three families, and the Russulineae with one.

The Aphyllophorales is also a large order, containing both fleshy fungi and minute plant pathogens; the Lycoperdales, containing the puffballs, is a relatively small order. The coral mushrooms, chanterelles, tooth fungi, and polypores are among the fungi which belong to the Aphyllophorales. Traditionally, six families of fungi were classified in the Aphyllophorales, but recent systems of classification split the order into 34 families. In this book, only six of the families, in which there are a number of species which produce large, fleshy sporocarps, are included.

list of genera, families, and orders. Every
genus included in the keys in this book is listed; the family to which it belongs is indicated by capital letters; *seg.* indicates segregate genera used by "splitters" in their systematic treatments.

The numbers in parentheses following the family designation refer to the total number of species in the genus and the number included in the keys in this book, respectively. NA= the number in North America; ca= circa or approximately.

Agaricaceae. Medium to large terrestrial mushrooms with free, or nearly free, close gills and dark spores. In most treatments, only one genus *Agaricus,* is included; in some treatements, *Lepiota* and *Chlorophyllum,* along with a number of segregate genera, are included. The family is primarily tropical in distribution; it is closely related to the Amanitaceae and Strophariaceae as well as the Lepiotaceae.

Agaricales. The order of fungi to which the gill mushrooms and boletes belong. The order is divided into three suborders, the Agaricineae, Boletineae, and Russulineae.

Agaricineae. A sub-order of the Agaricales consisting of eleven families: Hygrophoraceae, Tricholomataceae, Amanitaceae, Lepiotaceae, Agaricaceae, Strophariaceae, Coprinaceae, Bolbitiaceae, Cortinariaceae, Volvariaceae, and Entolomataceae.

Agaricus. (AGAR—40NA, 6) Medium to large, attractive, terrestrial fungi with free gills which are pinkish when young becoming chocolate brown to purplish brown with age; spore print chocolate brown often with purplish tints; stem central and easily separated from the cap; veil present forming a membranous ring, volva generally absent. Most of the species are edible; however, some species, having a phenol-like odor and/or white flesh which slowly turns yellow where bruised, are poisonous. The common cultivated mushroom is *A. bisporus.* (Seg. *Melanophyllum)*

Agrocybe. (BOLB—36, 2) Small to medium terrestrial mushrooms with brown gills and spore print and often brown caps and stems. They are hard to distinguish from other LBM's. Cap is convex to plane, dry or slightly tacky; stem is central, thick or thin and relatively fleshy; gills are attached. Spores are smooth, usually with a germ pore.

Albatrellus. (POLY—ca. 10, 2) Terrestrial polypores with convex to plane caps and minute pores which are usually decurrent; cap central or slightly off center. Spores very small, smooth, ellipsoid to nearly spherical, white.

Aleuria. (PEZI—ca. 10, 1)) Fleshy terrestrial cup fungi with relatively flat apothecia that are often brightly colored (orange to brown); flesh is brittle. The "orange peel" mushroom is often used raw in salads. The genus is often included in Peziza.

Amanita. (AMAN—60, 7) A genus of edible, non-edible, poisonous, and deadly poisonous mushrooms characterized by white, free gills, volva, annulus, white spore print, bulbous stem base, and a stately, attractive stature. Often the universal veil leaves patches of tissue on the cap in addition to a cup-like or merely scar-like volva. Some species and individual specimens in most species may lack one or two of these characteristics. Most fatal poisonings and many non-fatal poisonings are caused by *Amanitas.* Genus characteristics are further described in Chapter Three. (Seg. *Amidella, Amanitina, Amanitopsis, Amanitaria, Amplariella, Aspidella)*

Amanitaceae. Medium to large, stately mushrooms characterized by free, white or yellow gills, white spore print, and a universal veil which usually leaves remnants of tissue on the stem (the volva) or on the surface of the cap ("warts") or both. There are two genera in this family: *Amanita* and *Limacella.* The friesian genus *Vaginata* is now included in *Amanita.*

Amanitopsis = *Vaginata,* included under *Amanita.*

Aphyllophorales. Order to which Schizophyllaceae, Cantharellaceae, Hydnaceae, Polyporaceae, Clavariaceae, Thelephoraceae, and several families of non-fleshy fungi belong. Basidia are single celled; sporocarp development is gymnocarpous.

Armillaria. (TRIC—37, 5) Medium to large wood-inhabiting fungi growing as parasites on trees or as saprophytes on leaves, twigs, stumps, or logs. Can be distinguished from *Amanita* by its attached gills and from *Tricholoma* by the prominent annulus. Spores are white; stem is thick and often woody. There is no volva. (Seg. *Armillariella, Catathelasma)*

Astreus. (GEAS—2, 1) Medium to large earthstars in which the outer membrane ruptures in an irregular manner. Earthstars are too tough to be edible.

Auricularia. (AURI—15, 1) Jelly fungi with rather firm, leathery, ear-shaped sporocarps superficially similar to the sporocarps of *Peziza* but with the hymenium on the lower surface of the fruiting bodies. The species are easily cultivated and are the most important of the oriental mushrooms used for food.

Auriculariaceae. A family of saprophytic and parasitic fungi characterized by septate basidia and multicellular basidiospores. Genera include *Auricularia, Eocronartium, Jola, Herpobasidium,* and *Helicobasidium,* some species of which cause diseases of crops and ornamentals.

Auriculariales. The order to which the Auriculariaceae and Septobasidiaceae belong. It is closely related to the Tremellales.

Auriscalpium. (HYDN— 1, 1) Tooth fungi with leathery caps and long, laterally attached stem, growing on wood. Spores are somewhat rough.

Bolbitiaceae. A family of small, brown-spored mushrooms usually with brown cap, stem, and gills, distinguished from the Cortinariaceae by having a cellular cap cuticle and spores with an apical pore. Three genera are usually included in the family: *Bolbitius, Agrocybe,* and *Conocybe,* all with thin, cartilaginous stems. Species with free gills and thick, fleshy fibrous stems have been placed in *Pluteolus,* a Friesian genus now usually included in *Bolbitius.* Closely related to Coprinaceae.

Bolbitius (BOLB—6, 1) Small, brown mushrooms characterized by conspicuously striate, viscid caps and brown gills which are free from the stem at maturity and which often liquefy in wet weather. Stems are slender, fragile, and hollow. Neither ring nor volva is present.

Boletaceae. Fleshy, rapidly decaying mushrooms which resemble typical gill mushrooms but have the spores produced in tubes rather than on gills. The tube layer is thick and fleshy, not thin and woody as in the Polyporaceae. Two genera, *Boletus* and *Suillus,* are included in this book and are described in some detail in Chapter Four. It is closely related to the Gomphidiaceae and the Paxillaceae.

Boletineae. A sub-order of the Agaricales containing three families, the Boletaceae, Gomphidiaceae, and Paxillaceae.

Boletus. (BOLE—200, 21) A large genus of fleshy mushrooms usually forming mycorrhizae with conifers, oak and other trees; its characteristics are summarized in Chapter Four. The cep or king bolete *(B. edulis)* is one of the most prized of all mushrooms; the devil's bolete *(B. satanus),* on the other hand, is dangerously poisonous. (Seg. *Boletinus, Gyroporus, Leccinium, Porphyrellus, Pulveroboletus, Strobilomyces, Suillus, Gyrodon, Tylopilus,* and *Xerocomus)*

Calocera (TREM—ca. 5, 1) Small, brightly colored (yellow or orange), jelly fungi which resemble small coral fungi. Usually found on sticks or small logs in wooded areas.

Caloscypha. (AURI—2NA, 1) Yellow, leathery, jelly mushrooms which resemble cup fungi but have hymenium on undersurface of the cup. Common on leaf litter under conifers in the Rocky Mountains.

Calvatia. (LYCO–12, 4) Medium to very large terrestrial puff-balls which release their spores following disintegration of the upper part of the sporocarp. When cut longitudinally, a sterile base extends into the lower part of the sporocarp of most species. A species in which the capillitium has thorn-like branches is often placed in a separate genus, *Calbovista.*

Cantharellaceae. Mushrooms in which the hymenium is usually wrinkled or veined; sometimes the veins resemble gills, but they are connected by cross veins. Genera include *Cantharellus, Craterellus,* and *Comphus.* The family is very closely related to the Clavariaceae.

Cantharellus. (CANT—70, 9) Medium to large terrestrial mushrooms with prominent, often gill-like, veins which are dichotomously branched and connected by shallow cross veins. Margins are usually crenulate to lobed, cap is depressed and funnel-like, and the veins are decurrent. Spore print varies from white to yellow; caps are frequently yellow to orange. (Seg. *Cantharellula, Craterellus, Gomphus, Geopetalum, Hygrophoropsis, Leptoglossum,* and *Polyozellus)*

Chameota. (VOLV—3, 0) Rare mushrooms characterized by free gills, pink spore print, and ring but no volva.

Chlorophyllum (LEPI—ca. 5, 1) Large, attractive, terrestrial mushrooms, often 25—30 cm. in diameter, with white gills that turn green or buff with age; spore print green to buff; gills free from stem. Ring prominent and membranous; volva absent. Can be distinguished from *Lepiota* by the spore print, but not necessarily by the gill color. Poisonous.

Chroogomphus. (GOMP—ca. 10, 2) Medium-sized terrestrial mushrooms with decurrent gills, black spore print, and colored flesh. Superficially, they resemble chanterelles, but the cap is flat to convex, not depressed, and the gills are thin and wide. All of the known species are edible.

Clarkeinda. (LEPI— NA, 0) An asiatic tropical genus with olive green to purplish brown spore print characterized by both ring and volva.

Clavaria. (CLAV—80NA, 3) Small to medium terrestrial club fungi with white or pale ocher spore print and usually unbranched sporocarps. They differ from the chanterelles primarily in having a smooth or only very slightly wrinkled hymenium rather than decidedly wrinkled to vein-like. (Seg. *Clavariadelphus, Clavulinopsis, Clavulina, Ramariopsis, Ramaria*)

Clavariaceae. The club fungi and coral fungi, characterized by upright, often branching sporocarps with smooth to slightly wrinkled spore-bearing surface or hymenium. There are three genera (ignoring segregate genera): *Clavaria, Ramaria,* and *Sparassis.*

Clitocybe. (TRIC—80, 4) Small to large mushrooms with adnate to decurrent gills and thick, fleshy fibrous stems. Spore print is white to yellow. Caps and gills are usually gray to yellowish, sometimes white, and usually dry; they are not waxy like *Hygrophorus* and the stems are not brittle like *Russula.* Only a few species are edible, several are poisonous. (Seg. *Armillariella, Cantharellula, Laccaria, Lepista, Leucopaxillus, Lyophyllum, Hygrophoropsis, Omphalotus, Tricholomopsis)*

Clitopilus. (ENTO—11, 1) Medium-sized terrestrial mushrooms with fleshy fibrous stems, pink to red spore print, and decurrent gills. Cap is usually dry and smooth with a wavy margin and is often attached off center. While some of the species are edible and choice, they are easily confused with the deadly poisonous *Entolomas.* (Seg. *Entoloma, Rhodocybe,* and *Rhodophyllus)*

Collybia. (TRIC—40, 2) Minute to medium-sized woodland fungi that do not revive when moistened. Spore print white to pale buff, spores smooth, not amyloid. Stems thin cartilaginous; gill attachment usually notched, occasionally free or adnate; cap is typically convex to plane when mature with the margin inrolled when young. (Seg. *Baeospora, Callistosporium, Clitocybula, Fayodia, Flammulina, Lyophyllum, Marasmius, Oudemansiella, Podabrella, Pseudohiatula, Strobilurus,* and *Tricholomopsis)*

Conocybe. (BOLB—25, 1) Fragile little brown mushrooms found in grass, dung, and moss. Caps sharply conical to bell shaped; gills brown, adnexed to almost free; stems very thin, cartilaginous, hollow, with or without a ring. Caps are neither striate nor translucent, as a rule. Some of the species contain amanitin, the same toxin that occurs in the *Amanita phalloides* and *Galerina venenata* complexes and none of them is large enough to be edible even if they weren't potentially dangerous. Typically the sporocarps appear in the morning of a hot summer day and have shriveled up by late afternoon.

Coprinaceae. Fragile mushrooms with purple-brown to black spores and thin, cartilaginous stems. A volva or a ring, but not both, is sometimes present. The gills are free, adnexed, or sometimes adnate, but never decurrent. There are four genera: *Coprinus, Panaeolus, Hypholoma,* and *Psathyrella.* The family is closely related to the Bolbitiaceae and probably the Strophariaceae.

Coprinus. (COPR—12, 7) Small to medium mushrooms with pink gills that turn black and then usually deliquesce. The genus is described in Chapter Four. (Seg. *Pseudocoprinus*)

Cortinariaceae. A very large family of small to large mushrooms with brown spore print and usually brown gills; caps and stems are also frequently brown. The family is discussed in Chapter Four. The Cortinariaceae are similar to the Bolbitiaceae but are typically cool weather fungi whereas the latter are warm weather fungi. Most "LBM's" belong to this family. Because of its size, it is divided into seven tribes. The tribes, with their most common genera (ignoring segregate genera) are (1) Cortinarieae with *Cortinarius, Phaeocollybia, Galerina, Gymnopilis,* and *Rozites;* (2) Crepioteae with *Pleurotellus* and *Crepidotus;* (3) Inocybeae with *Inocybe, Hebeloma, Naucoria,* and *Simocybe;* (4) Phaeolepioteae with *Phaeolepiota* and *Descolea;* (5) Pholiotoideae with *Pholiota;* (6) Ripartiteae with *Ripartites;* and (7) Tubarieae with *Tubaria* and *Flammulaster.* Both edible and poisonous species occur in the family; some species are deadly poisonous.

Cortinarius. (CORT—1000, 7) Medium to large mushrooms with brown spore print, thick, fleshy fibrous stems, gills adnate to almost free, and a spider web-like cortina often reaching from the young cap to the stem. There is no volva present, but the cortina may leave a ring of hairs on the stem. Caps may be blue, purple, red, yellow, white, or other colors. The rust colored spore print helps to distinguish *Cortinarius* from *Hebeloma* and *Inocybe.* For species identification, young sporocarps are needed so that gill color and cortina characteristics can be noted. (Seg. *Dermocybe, Leprocybe, Myxacium, Orelani, Phlegmacium, Sericeocybe,* and *Telamonia*)

Craterellus. (CANT—20, 1) Chanterelle-like fungi with short, discontinuous veins (gills) or with a smooth or slightly wrinkled hymenium, like a club fungus. Caps are trumpet-shaped with very wavy margins and decurrent gills; the spore print is white to buff.

Crepidotus. (CORT—125NA, 1) Small to medium-sized fungi, with brown spores, growing shelf-like on wood; caps round to kidney-shaped, attached by a short stem or plug or directly by the margin. Spore print cinnamon brown. Absence of stem distinguishes it from Paxillus. (Seg. *Melanotus, Phaeomarasmius, Pleuroflammula, Pleurotellus, Pyrrhoglossum, Simocybe)*

Cyathus. (NIDU—40, 1) Small birds-nest fungi; exterior of nest shaggy, interior often striate or fluted; eggs small (1–2 mm.), gray to black; spores large (ca. 20-30 mu.); nest three layered.

Cystoderma. (TRIC—14NA, 1) Small woodland fungi with white spores, adnexed to adnate gills, and thick, fleshy fibrous stems. Caps and stems are typically brown coated with a layer of mealy or powdery granules. Spores are small, smooth, and usually amyloid.

Dacrymyces. (TREM—ca. 15, 1) Bright yellow or orange jelly fungi characterized by soft, gelatinous fruiting bodies composed of dicaryotic hyphae of very small diameter completely surrounded by a gelatinous coating in which the spores accumulate, sliding down this when it becomes wet. Traditionally placed in the Tremellaceae of the Tremellales, these fungi are now often segregated into their own family in the Exobasidiales.

Discina. (PEZI—2, 2) Brittle, leathery disk fungi, usually with a stem. The apothecium is flat or disk-shaped, occasionally slightly convex or concave, with a wrinkled upper surface. Both species are generally reported to be edible; they are sometimes regarded as variants of a single species.

Echinodontium. (HYDN—1, 1) Woody, hoof-shaped "conk" on conifer trees. The sporocarp resembles a *Fomes* but has stout, gray teeth. Spore print white.

Endoptychum. (HYME—ca. 5, 2) Puffball-like mushrooms with differentiated gleba resembling the gills of an unopened *Agaricus;* stem present.

Entoloma. (ENTO—200NA, 4) Attractive, medium-sized

mushrooms characterized by pink, flesh-colored, or salmon gills attached to but usually almost free from the fleshy fibrous, or sometimes cartilaginous, stem; spores pink to red, angular; no volva; no ring, except in three tropical species. Some species are **deadly** poisonous. (Seg. *Nolanea, Lepista, Claudopus, Alboleptonia;* synonym: Rhodophyllus)

Entolomataceae. Small to fairly large mostly terrestrial fungi with dry to slightly viscid cap usually attached to stem centrally; gills attached but sometimes seceding; ring and volva absent; spore print red or pink, spores angular or longitudinally ridged, not amyloid. Genera included are *Claudopus, Clitopilus, Nolanea, Leptonia,* and *Entoloma.* Synonym: *Rhodophyllaceae.*

Fistulina. (POLY—1, 1) The "beefsteak" or "ox tongue" fungus so called because the sporocarp resembles an ox tongue. Cap is 7 to 30 cm. broad, reddish orange becoming dark red or liver-colored; flesh thick, succulent, ooze a dark reddish juice when fresh. Spore print pink to pale rusty brown. Stem short or absent. The tubes are free, not united as in other polypores and in the boletes.

Fomes. (POLY—120, 68NA, 2) Woody polypores forming "conks" on trees, stumps, and logs. The sporocarps are perennial and a new, thin, layer of tubes is produced each year; conks with 60 or 70 "growth rings" have been found. *Fomes* is distinguished from many of the other hardy, woody, perennial polypores by its white, rather than brown, spore print.

Galerina. (CORT—200NA, 4) Minute to small LBM's with spore print some shade of brown; thin, cartilaginous stems; gills adnexed to adnate, brown; ring oblique, relatively obscure or absent; volva absent. Several species contain significant quantities of amanitin and are therefore deadly poisonous. The caps are generally more rounded than those of *Conocybe,* are often mammillate, and are smooth. *Galerina* spp. are found mostly on rotting wood or in wet grass or moss, occasionally on the soil. Formerly most species were included in *Pholiota* or in the obsolete (illegitimate) genus *Galera.*

Geastraceae. Puffballs in which the outer layer of wall tissue splits longitudinally in a more or less regular manner and then open up to form a star-like structure beneath the rest of the sporocarp. Though not poisonous, none of the earthstars are edible because of the tough walls. There are two common genera: *Astreus* and *Geastrum.*

Geastrum. (GEAS—30, 2) Earthstars in which the outer skin or wall of the sporocarps splits longitudinally in a regular manner to form radially symmetrical stars in the center of which is the remainder of the puffball.

Gomphidiaceae. Gill mushrooms of the sub-order Boletineae, order Agaricales, characterized by decurrent gills, thick fleshy fibrous stems, and smoky black spore print. The spores are spindle shaped (boletoid) or long and narrowly elliptical; the species are mycorrhizal and are often associated with species of *Suillus.* There are two genera, *Chroogomphus* and *Gomphidius;* there are no known poisonous species.

Gomphidius. (GOMP—20, 4) Gomphidiaceae in which the flesh is white. The decurrent gills and smoky black spore print are distinguishing characteristics. (Seg. *Cystogomphus* and *Chroogomphus)*

Gomphus. Included here in *Cantharellus.* It is sometimes allied with other chanterelles and placed in a separate family, the Gomphaceae.

Gymnopilus. (CORT—75 NA, 1) Medium to large fungi found mostly on wood. Cap dry, smooth or scaly, bright yellow to reddish brown; gills notched to slightly decurrent, usually yellow to rusty orange; stem thick, fleshy fibrous, usually with a ring; volva absent. They are easily confused with *Pholiota;* however, the spore print has a strong orange tint which is lacking in *Pholiota* and also in *Hebeloma* and *Inocybe.* None of the species are of much value as edibles, but several species are reported to contain appreciable quantities of nerve type poisons.

Gyromitra. (HELV—11, 3) Medium to large sac fungi in which the apothecium is curved back over the stem; the hymenium is wrinkled or convoluted so that the sporocarp resembles a brain. Caps are tan to dark brown; stems are brittle, hollow, or almost absent. These are cold weather mushrooms appearing early in the spring and in the mountains near snow banks. Several species contain appreciable quantities of gyromitrin, a protoplasmic type toxin, and should never be eaten without first parboiling; no Gyromitra should ever be eaten raw.

Hebeloma. (CORT—15, 3) Medium-sized mushrooms with brown spore print and usually brown gills and light brownish cap and stem, growing on soil in forested areas or sometimes on cultivated land. Cap usually smooth, sticky or slightly slimy when moist, flat to convex, margin sometimes inrolled; gills adnate to adnexed; stem fleshy fibrous. Flesh, when cap is broken and crushed, often smells like radishes. All of the species which have been tested are poisonous. The smooth, slightly viscid cap and the dull brown, not rusty, spores help to differentiate the *Hebelomas* from the *Inocybes* and *Cortinarii.*

Helvella. (HELV—ca. 30, 6) Medium-sized sac fungi in which the apothecium is curved back over the stem; the hymenium is smooth or slightly wrinkled and the cap often resembles a miniature saddle, both in shape and in color. Stems are brittle and hollow. Apparently some species contain significant amounts of gyromitrin; *Helvella* species should never be eaten raw. (Seg. *Gyromitra, Underwoodia*)

Helvellaceae. Sac fungi in which the apothecium is curved back over the stem; stems are usually hollow and brittle. Most members of the family contain small to large quantities of gyromitrin, a water soluble, volatile toxin which can be removed by parboiling or, in many cases, by cooking. Gyromitrin hydrolizes to monomethylhydrazine (MMH), a carcinogenic toxin which is deadly poisonous in relatively small doses; inhalation of the vapors from parboiling mushrooms can be dangerous; drinking the water in which mushrooms were parboiled can be fatal. If cooked in a covered container, the MMH will not escape and the mushroom may be as dangerous as if eaten raw. MMH is used in the manufacture of rocket fuel. Genera include the true morels (*Morchella* and *Verpa*), the false morels (*Helvella* and *Gyromitra*), *Underwoodia,* and *Daleomyces.*

Hericium. (HYDN—ca. 50, 2) Tooth fungi in which the sporocarp is attached directly to a trunk, stump, or log. The sporocarp is usually a soft, fragile, white mass of tissue with relatively long (up to 70 mm.) spines; spore print white. None of the *Hericiums* are poisonous.

Hydnaceae. The tooth fungi. A family of the Aphyllophoorales in which the spores are borne on the outer surface of projecting spines. Genera include *Auriscalpium, Hericium, Hydnellum, Hydnum,* and *Phellodon.*

Hydnellum. (HYDN—ca. 60, 1) Terrestrial fungi with teeth or warts on the undersurface of the cap; stem short or absent; flesh tough. Caps large (>4 cm.), teeth blunt, spore print brown.

Hydnum. (HYDN—120, 7) Terrestrial fungi with soft, brittle flesh, soft spines on undersurface of an often scaly cap. Spore print white or brown; those with white spore print are often placed in a separate genus, *Dentinum.* (Seg. *Hericium, Hydnellum, Dentinum*)

Hygrophoraceae. Gill mushrooms characterized by white spore print and soft, thick, waxy gills that are usually widely spaced. The cap is usually thick and fleshy fibrous, without ring or volva. One genus: *Hygrophorus.*

Hygrophorus. (HYGR—244NA, 7) Small to medium-sized terrestrial mushrooms with white spores and attached gills (adnexed to decurrent) which may become free at maturity; stem fleshy fibrous, lacking ring and volva. Caps are sometimes white, often brightly colored, conical to mammilate, convex, or plane. Except for spore differences and the waxy appearance and feel to the gills (caused by the spores), they are difficult to distinguish from *Clitocybe, Laccaria,* and *Tricholoma* in the Tricholomataceae. Several of the species are edible but generally not highly prized; a few species are poisonous but none seriously so. (Seg. *Aeruginospora, Camarophyllus, Humidocutis, Hygroaster, Hygrocybe,* and *Neohygrophorus*)

Hymenogastraceae. Medium sized fungi most often buried or partially buried in humus; stem usually absent or rudimentary, sporocarp usually globose. Many resemble puffballs, but the capillitium is absent; they also superficially resemble truffles (genus Tuber) and many of them are called "false truffles." Among the genera included are the following: *Arcangeliella,*

Endoptychum, Hydnangium, Hymenogaster, Macowanites, Melanogaster Rhizopogon, and *Secotium.* Very few species are edible.

Hymenogastrales. The order to which the Hymenogastraceae and several other families of fungi belong including the Proto-gastraceae, Hemigastraceae, and Sclerodermataceae. There is wide difference of opinion among mycologists as to how the traditional members of the Hymenogastrales should be classified and how the different genera have evolved and are related to each other.

Hypholoma (COPR—ca. 10, 1) Generally considered to be a synonym of *Psathyrella;* when they are separated, these are *Psathyrella*-like mushrooms with a combination of purple-brown spore print, especially fragile, hollow stems, and growing in grassy habitats rather than on logs or stumps.

Inocybe. (CORT—70, 4) Small to medium-size, ill-smelling mushrooms found on very rotten wood or on soil; the cap is typically silky, minutely scaly, or woolly, usually mammillate; stems are usually fleshy fibrous, sometimes thin and cartilaginous, with gills adnate to nearly free, but decurrent in some species, usually brown; there is no volva; ring, if present, is obscure. *Inocybes* are difficult to distinguish from each other and also from *Hebelomas* and *Galerinas;* since all known species of *Inocybe* and *Hebeloma* are poisonous and several species of *Galerina* are deadly poisonous, mycophagists label them LBM's and move on. (Seg. *Clypeus = Astrosporina*)

Laccaria. (TRIC—10, 2) Small to medium-sized terrestrial fungi with dry, plane to convex cap with slightly wavy margin; pink or flesh-colored to purple, thick, slightly waxy, attached gills that are usually rather widely spaced; and very tough, fibrous, long and slender stem lacking both ring and volva. Spore print white to pale lilac; spores usually spiny. The sporocarps dry in place rather than decompose; therefore this rather common genus appears to be even more common than it is; it is especially common on sandy soil under pines and occurs in sand dunes. There are no reports of toxins in the genus; some species are rated by some mycophagists as good to choice.

Lactarius. (RUSS—200NA, 12) Young specimens are readily

identified by the milky fluid which is exuded when the stem or cap is cut or broken; older specimens may be confused with *Russula;* however the gills are usually colored (orange, green, etc.) while the gills of *Russula* are usually white to yellow, sometimes discoloring in age or where bruised to dull reds, browns, or black; also the stems of *Lactarius* are often hollow. The genus is further described in Chapter Four.

LBM. Little brown mushrooms: members of the Cortinariaceae Bolbitiaceae, Tricholomataceae, and other families having small sporocarps with brown caps, stems, and/or gills that are difficult to distinguish from each other. Most LBM's are brown or some shade of brown, such as buff, dingy white, or dismal gray, but some are just a nondescript though dull color.

Lentinus. (TRIC—9, 2) Medium to large mushrooms growing on wood with centrally attached or sometimes eccentric stems. Characterized by white spore print, fleshy fibrous, often woody stems, and decurrent gills which are serrate or crenulate. The scaly caps and serrate to crenulate gills are usually enough to identify this genus. None of the species are known to be poisonous although some are either very bitter or peppery; two species, *Lentinus lepideus* (at least some strains of it) and the shiitake, *L. edodes* are edible and good to choice. (Seg. *Lentinellus, Nothopanus, Panus,* and *Pleurotus*)

Lepiota. (LEPI—ca. 100, 5) Medium-sized or small terrestrial fungi especially abundant in the tropics but with many species in temperate regions. The cap is dry, usually scaly around the edges, and separates cleanly from the stem; gills are free, close, white in young specimens soon turning tan to buff; the stem is typically clavate (swollen near the base) but lacks a volva; the ring is usually prominent, membranous or hairy, and often becomes free from the stem so that it can slide up and down the typically hollow stem. Spore print is white to pale buff. Both edible and poisonous species occur, but because of the danger of confusion with *Amanita* great caution is advised before eating any *Lepiota.* (Seg. *Chamaemyces, Chlorophyllum, Cystolepiota, Leucoagaricus, Leucocoprinus, Limacella, Macrolepiota, Melanophyllum, Pseudobaeospora, Smithiomyces, Termitomyces*)

Lepiotaceae. Small to relatively large terrestrial mushrooms common in lawns and meadows characterized by free gills, white to green spore print, and prominent ring but no volva. Two genera are included, *Lepiota* and *Chlorophyllum*. The species superficially resemble the Amanitaceae and the two families are combined by some taxonomists; however, basic anatomical differences suggest that the similarities are only analogous. The family is closely related to the Agaricaceae and like it is primarily tropical in distribution.

Leptonia. *Entolomas* with flat or depressed caps and thin, cartilaginous stems.

Limacella. (AMAN—12, 0) Rare, medium-sized mushrooms with white spore print characterized by a universal veil that turns into a mass of slime at the base of the stem instead of a volva. The viscid to slimy cap and slimy stem base should be sufficient to distinguish this genus from *Lepiota*. Presence or absence of toxins has not been reported for any of the species and it would be very unwise to experiment with this genus.

Lycoperdaceae. The puffballs, mushrooms characterized by a gleba consisting of a network of threads called the capillitium and a homogenous tissue which differentiate into spores surrounded by a double wall of tissue which hold the spores in place until they are discharged into the air either by disintegration of the upper portion of the walls or through an ostiole or pore at the sporocarp apex. The capillitium is microscopic; therefore, sectioning the sporocarp longitudinally reveals a very homogeneous mass of tissue which distinguishes the puffballs from truffles, false truffles, and button stage agarics. There are two genera: *Calvatia* and *Lycoperdon*.

Lycoperdales. The order to which the puffballs and earth stars belong. There are two families, the Lycoperdaceae and Geastraceae.

Lycoperdon. (LYCO—50, 4) The "true puffballs" or mushrooms in which the spores escape from the sporocarp through an opening at the apex of the fruit. The force exerted by a grasshopper landing on a mature puffball or by falling hail or rain is sufficient to send up a cloud of black "smoke" consisting of millions of spores. Puffballs are further discussed in Chapter Two. (Seg. *Bovista, Calvatia, Calbovista*)

Lyophyllum. (TRIC—25, 1) Small to medium-sized terrestrial mushrooms typically growing in large clumps characterized by white spores which are borne on basidia that stain red when heated in acetocarmine. In gross morphology the genus is highly variable, even though consistent in microscopic features. Our most common species are distinguished from *Tricholoma, Clitocybe,* and *Collybia* by the soapy feeling to the cap and the large clumps they grow in, and from *Entoloma* by spore color and shape. (Seg. *Asterophora* and *Calocybe*)

Macowanites. (HYME—1, 1) A desert "puffball" with a short stalk; when cut longitudinally, the sporocarp can be seen to be differentiated into an internal stalk and convoluted gill-like structures. The stem is thick and brittle, as in *Russula,* and the spore mass is white to yellow with sphaerocysts present. It has been suggested that the genus was based on an aberrant specimen of *Russula* or other gill mushroom and should be declared illegitimate; however, the only species, though not common, is occasionally found. It is reported to be edible.

Marasmius. (TRIC—185, 4) Small to minute fungi with plane to convex, brownish caps and pallid, well-spaced gills which are usually adnate to almost free, occasionally decurrent. The stem is thin, tough, and cartilaginous or wiry; neither ring or volva is present; spore print is white, spores are smooth. *Marasmius* species are easily distinguished from *Mycena, Collybia,* and *Omphalina* by their ability when completely dry to fully revive when placed in water; also, the cap is flatter than *Mycena* caps and lacks the inrolled margin typical of *Collybia* and *Omphalina.* Most species are too small to bother collecting for table use, but some are edible and choice. Care must be exercised, however, to avoid confusion with poisonous *Clitocybes* or untested, and possibly poisonous, *Collybias.* (Seg. *Collybia, Crinipellis, Marasmiellus, Micromphale, Mycenella,* and *Xeromphalina*)

Morchella. (HELV—15, 6) Medium to large sac fungi in which the apothecium grows back over the stem to form a large, sponge-shaped cap; the hymenium consists of squarish pits rather than wrinkles or convolutions as in the false morels (*Gyromitra* and *Helvella*). The genus is further discussed in Chapter Two under the "foolproof four."

Mutinus. (PHAL—10, 1) A puffball-like fungus in which the interior of the ball, or "egg," is differentiated into a stem with mature spores; at full maturity, the stem expands, rupturing the egg, and an erect, hollow, pointed stem covered with green slime containing spores results. The foul odor attracts flies which spread the spores. The genus is distinguished from *Phallus* by its lack of a cap or head at the apex of the stem.

Mycena. (TRIC—218NA, 3) Small to minute saprophytic fungi with conical to campanulate or mammilate caps, usually translucent and striate, and thin, fragile, hollow cartilaginous stems; unlike *Marasmius*, the sporocarps do not revive when placed in water. Spore print is white; spores are smooth. Sporocarps are usually gray or brown, but a few species are brightly colored. Most species are too small to be considered edible; those known to be edible are easily confused with other, possibly poisonous, Tricholomataceae. (Seg. *Delicatula, Fayodia, Hydropus, Hemimycena, Mycenella,* and *Pseudohiatula*)

Naematoloma. (STRO—15, 3) Small to medium-sized mushrooms found mostly on wood; caps smooth, brightly colored; stem slender but fleshy fibrous; gills attached, dark at maturity; spore print deep brown to purple-brown. The dry, often brightly colored caps, and the lack of an annulus help distinguish these mushrooms from the *Stropharias*; the fleshy fibrous, rather than cartilaginous stem, and tough, rather than fragile, flesh help to distinguish them from *Psathyrellas*. Some species are poisonous, and are reported to have caused deaths, although they are so bitter that it is difficult to imagine anyone eating enough to be fatal; other species are edible but considered mediocre, or too bitter to eat. Some of the species were formerly classified in *Hypholoma*.

Naucoria. (CORT—100, 0) Small to minute "LBM's" with gills adnexed to adnate; otherwise similar in appearance to *Tubaria*.

Nidularia. (NIDU—5, 0) The true bird's nest fungi belong to this genus; it differs from *Cyathus* in that the nest is two layered instead of three, the eggs are lighter colored and they lack a funiculus, or cord, but are sticky instead. None of the species are large enough to be considered edible; the nest and eggs are also too tough to eat. (Seg. *Nidula, Mycocalia, Crucibulum*)

Nidulariaceae. A family of five genera *(Cyathus, Crucibulum, Mycocalia, Nidula,* and *Nidularia*) in which the sporocarp consists of two parts, an outer wall which at maturity is open, and one or more glebal chambers, called peridioles, which resemble eggs within a nest. In some genera, each peridiole is attached to a funiculus which attaches to stems or blades of grass and thus aid in dispersion. The family is closely related to the Lycoperdaceae and the Sphaerobolaceae.

Nidulariales. This is the order of fungi to which the bird's nest fungi belong. There are two families, the Nidulariaceae and the Sphaerobolaceae. None of the species are large or succulent enough to be edible.

Nolanea. *Entolomas* having conical instead of convex caps and cartillaginous instead of fleshy stems.

Omphalotus. (TRIC—ca. 10, 1) Brightly colored, wood-inhabiting mushrooms with decurrent gills that luminesce when fresh; stem central or slightly eccentric with neither annulus nor volva, fleshy fibrous; spore print white, spores smooth. The decurrent, yellow to bright orange gills, that are usually olive tinted, and the smooth cap and stem are generally sufficient to set this genus apart; the bright colors and olive tinted gills help to distinguish it from *Clitocybe* with which it intergrades. All of the known species are poisonous.

Omphalina. (TRIC—12, 2) Small to minute dainty, usually brightly colored mushrooms with plane or depressed caps with incurved margins when young; decurrent, yellow or orange gills; thin, tough cartilaginous stems lacking ring and volva; spore print white to pale yellow. They are usually found on moss, in grass, or on soggy logs; several species grow only with lichens. They most nearly resemble species of Mycena but never have a conical or a mammillate cap. They are too small to eat. (Seg. *Clitocybula, Delicatula, Fayodia, Hemimycena, Hydropus, Gerronema, Lyophyllum,*

Leptogoglossum, Mycena, Neoclitocybe, Omphalia, Pseudoomphalina, and *Xeromphalina*)

Osteina. (POLY—1,1) Hard, woody shelf fungi characterized by the base of the sporocarps persisting to form a gnarled, underground, stem-like structure that holds the overlapping shelves together.

Panaeolus. (COPR—7, 4) Dung inhabiting attractive mushrooms with purplish brown to black spore print and black gills; stems are thin and cartilaginous, with or without an annulus, lacking a volva. In contrast to *Coprinus,* the gills are mottled and do not deliquesce or change color as they age. Some mycologists place the species with purple-brown spore print in the genus *Psathyrella.* The genus is further described in Chapter Four. There are several poisonous species in the genus; and at least one edible species. (Seg. *Annellaria, Copelandia,* and *Panaeolina*)

Panus. (TRIC—ca. 15, 0) Usually included in either *Lentinus* or *Pleurotus,* it differs from the former in having entire gill edges and from the latter in being woody rather than fleshy. Although some species are edible, most are too woody to be of any great culinary value. (Seg. *Asterotus, Lentinus, Nothopanus, Pleurotus, Panellus,* and *Tectella*)

Paxillaceae. A family of gill mushrooms characterized by white, mustard yellow, or yellow-brown spores, similar to bolete spores, and gills which become vein-like, or sometimes pore-like, near the stem. It is included in the sub-order Boletineae of the Agaricales. Some mycologists include three genera in the family: *Paxillus, Phylloporus,* and *Hygrophoropsis;* others lump all three in *Paxillus.*

Paxillus. (PAXI—5 NA, 2) Medium sized mushrooms growing on wood or on the ground near stumps, characterized by decurrent gills, mustard yellow to yellow-brown spore print (white in *P. aurantiacus*), and usually off center or marginal attachment of stem (if present) to cap. It is readily distinguished from most species of *Crepidotus* since *Crepidotus* always attaches by the margin without a stem whereas *Paxillus* usually has at least a short stem attached more or less centrally and the margin of the cap is often strongly inrolled. Although some of the species are edible, they are very poisonous raw or improperly cooked. (Seg. *Hygrophoropsis, Lepista, Linderomyces, Phylloporus,* and *Ripartites*)

Peziza. (PEZI—50, 2) Ascomycetes with brittle to somewhat leathery flesh, and cup-like to disk-like apothecia usually attached directly to the substrate without a stem. *Peziza* includes brownish species; the brightly colored species are usually placed in other genera. (Seg. *Aleuria, Discina, Sarcosphaera*)

Pezizaceae. A large family of sac fungi in which the sporocarps are fleshy to leathery, but not carbonaceous, and disk-shaped to cup-shaped. They grow on soil, humus, dung, or wood. The asci (spore sacs) contain eight spores and open by means of a lid at the apex. Some taxonomists split the genera into many smaller genera and group these in a number of tribes; one recent book places all of the species in four genera. Some of the genera usually included in the family are *Aleuria, Anthracobia, Discina, Patella, Peziza, Rhizina, Sarcosphaera,* and *Scutellinia.*

Pezizales. A large order of fleshy ascomycetes to which the families Sarcoscyphaceae, Pezizaceae, Ascobolaceae, and Helvellaceae belong.

Phaeocollybia. (CORT—ca. 15, 1) Medium-sized terrestrial mushrooms of forested areas, especially douglas-fir and redwood. They are characterized by the almost free gills, rusty brown to cinnamon brown spore print, and base of stem tapering into a long, fine pseudorhiza or "taproot;" there is neither a ring nor a volva.

Phallaceae. The "stinkhorns," a group of fleshy fungi that superfically resemble puffballs when immature, but in which the "puffball" contains an internal stem and spores; as the internal stem expands, the structure then typically resembles an ascomycete with a long thick stem and small cap. The family contains about ten genera: *Aporophallus, Dictyophora, Echinophallus, Floccomutinus, Itajahya, Jansia, Mutinus, Phallus, Staheliomyces,* and *Xylophagus;* only four of the genera occur in North America.

Phallales. The order to which the stinkhorns belong. There are two families in most treatments of the order, the Clathraceae and the Phallaceae.

Phallus. (PHAL—10, 2) Stinkhorns lacking a skirt and

possessing a head or enlarged area at the apex of the internal stem. Because of their putrid odor, they are seldom eaten; most species that have been eaten, usually as pickled "eggs," are reported to be non-poisonous. One species—its identification uncertain—seems to have been responsible for a non-fatal poisoning of a young lady in England.

Phellodon. (HYDN—ca. 15, 1) Tooth fungi having tough flesh and white spores. They are small to medium terrestrial mushrooms with cap and stem, growing singly or in large groups in which the caps may fuse into one duplex mass; stem is well developed, attached centrally or somewhat eccentrically; odor is usually fragrant.

Phlogiotis. (TREM—1, 1) Jelly fungi in which the sporocarp develops into a tall (10—12 cm.) funnel shaped cap with spores on the under or outer surface. At first glance it resembles a false morel. *P. helvelloides* is candied or pickled and usually considered the best of the jelly fungi.

Pholiota. (CORT—200NA, 13) Medium sized mushrooms found on wood or wood debris; cap scaly or viscid; stem fleshy fibrous, usually with a persistent, membranous or fibrillose ring; volva absent, stem often scaly below the ring; gills adnexed or almost free to adnate, occasionally slightly decurrent; spore print brown to rusty brown. *Pholiota* species usually resemble *Naematoloma, Stropharia, Gymnopilus,* and *Agaricus,* but can be recognized by careful observation of spore print color and gill characteristics. Most species are edible but not many are especially good; a few are mildly poisonous. They are abundant on coniferous slash. (Seg. *Agrocybe, Flammula, Galerina, Hebeloma, Inocybe, Kuehneromyces, Phaeolepiota, Phaeomarasmius, Pholiotina*)

Pleurotus. (TRIC—60, 3) All of the fleshy white spored mushrooms with decurrent gills attached by the margin or a short, plug-like stem to wood are traditionally placed in this genus; woody species are now often segregated as the genus *Panus.* Even with these species removed, the genus is undoubtedly an artificial assemblage of unrelated species needing further splitting. (Seg. *Anthracophyllum, Chaetocolathus, Cheimonophyllum, Gerronema, Hohenbuehelia, Hypizygus, Lampteromyces, Lentinellus, Lentinus,*

Leptoglossum, Lyophyllum, Nothopanus, Panellus, Phyllotopsis, Pleuro-cybella, Pleurocollybia, Pleurotellus, Resupinatus, Rhodotus, and *Tricholomopsis.*)

Pluteolus. (BOLB—ca. 5, 1) Small brown mushrooms with free gills and brown spores. Any mushroom with brown spore print in which the gills are completely free of the stem while the sporocarp is young should belong to this genus—or subgenus. *Pluteolus* is generally included in *Bolbitius* in modern taxonomic systems, usually as a subgenus; it differs from the rest of the genus in that the gills are completely free in the young sporocarps.

Pluteus. (VOLV—40, 3) Small to medium-sized wood inhabiting mushrooms with pink spore print and free gills; stem may be either fleshy fibrous or cartilaginous, volva and ring are both absent. Spores ellipsoid and smooth. None of the species are known to be poisonous and the larger species are edible and very good. The sporocarps decompose rapidly. They can be distinguished from the deadly *Entolomas* by their free gills, but care must be taken to be sure the gills actually are free and microscopic examination of the spores is advised; *Pluteus* has smooth, ellipsoid spores while *Entoloma* has angular spores.

Podaxaceae. A small family of desert and tropical mushrooms in which the mature sporocarps resemble unopened buttons of Agaricales. Only one genus is included, *Podaxis.*

Podaxales. The order to which the Podaxaceae belong.

Podaxis. (PODA—30, 1) A small genus of tropical and desert mushrooms in which the puffball-like sporocarp is differentiated internally into stem and gill-like structures. *Podaxis pistillaris* resembles a young shaggy mane, but the spores are never exposed to the air until conditions for germination are right. Spores have very thick walls, further protecting their contents from dessication in the desert heat.

Polyporaceae. A large family of bracket fungi and related plants, most of which are tough and woody. Most species grow on wood, often as parasites on living trees where they form "conks" which weaken and gradually decompose the wood. At one time the family included the Boletes and other fungi with pores; now it is limited to the bracket and related fungi most of which produce white spores. For species having brown, purple, or other colored spores, see the Thelephoraceae. Genera include *Albatrellus*, *Fomes*, *Polyporus*, *Poria*, *Osteina*, *Fistulina*, and others. *Fistulina* is sometimes placed in a family by itself.

Polyporus. (POLY—300, 6) Wood inhabiting bracket fungi in which new sporocarps are produced annually from the perennial mycelium by means of a simple, unbranched stalk; flesh is less woody than in many polypores, light colored or white, and succulent; pores are round or somewhat elongated, much smaller than in the boletes but large enough to be seen without a hand lens or microscope; spores are white. (Seg. *Fomes*, *Albatrellus*, *Ganoderma*, *Poria*, *Cryptoporus*, *Grifola*, and others)

Psalliota = *Agaricus*

Psathyrella. (COPR—400NA, 2) Small to medium-sized mushrooms found mostly on wood or in humus; cap conical to convex or plane, typically some shade of brown, buff, or gray; flesh very fragile, gills dark brown to black at maturity, usually attached but not decurrent; spore print purple-brown to black; however, the species with purple-brown spore print are sometimes placed in *Hypholoma*, especially if the stem is fleshy fibrous. *Psathyrella* grows on well-rotted wood; *Panaeolus* grows on fresh cow or horse manure; where both are growing on grass, the former will have a convex to flat cap while the latter will have a conical to bell-shaped cap. By paying special attention to the substrate on which they are growing, it should be possible to distinguish between them. While some of the species are edible, there are many potentially poisonous species in the genus and it is recommended that you do not experiment with them or even eat those that are *believed* to be edible.

Pseudohydnum. (TREM—1, 1) Jelly fungi in which the undersurface of the sporocarp is covered with tooth-like pro-tuberances. When young, the sporocarp, consisting of cap and stem, is somewhat hard and dry, but as it matures, it becomes jelly-like, apparently due to deliquescence of the internal hyphae. *P. gelatinosum* is often marinated and used in salads; it is also frequently eaten with honey and cream and reported to be good.

Psilocybe. (STRO—30, 3) Any little brown mushroom having purple-gray to purple-brown spore sprint, cartilaginous stem, attached gills, and meets, in addition, one of the following criteria— base of the stem and/or upper stem or cap turning blue or green where bruised; or growing on dung; or growing on grass, moss, or humus and having a conical to mammilate cap—is a species of *Psilocybe*. If the base of stem or the cap turns blue or green when bruised (due to oxidation of psilocin), the species is poisonous. At least ten species of *Psilocybe* are much sought after because of the hallucinogenic toxins they contain; *Psilocybe cubensis* and *P. mexicana* are probably the most important species used in Indian religious ceremonies involving intoxication by hallucinogenic drugs. (Seg. *Naematoloma, Panaeolina,* and *Psathyrella*)

Ramaria. (CLAV—70, 9) Coral fungi having profusely branched sporocarps that are often brightly colored; spore print yellowish to ocherous. The branches are generally erect and smooth, never ribbon-like, and usually arise from a fleshy base; their similarity to coral is usually enough to identify them as *Ramaria* species. One or two species are poisonous, but not dangerously so; most of the others are edible. (Seg. *Clavicorona, Ramariopsis, Clavulina*)

Rhizina. (PEZI—2, 1) Fruiting body very dark, flattened, amorphous; attached to soil by root-like "rhizines" consisting of interwoven hyphae. Grows on needles and conifer debris following fire, fruiting in early spring and late fall. Some mycologists place *Rhizina* in the Helvellaceae instead of Pezi-zaceae.

Rhizopogon. (HYME—15, 1) Spherical, subterranean mush-rooms which resemble truffles or some puffballs, until they are sectioned. In contrast to puffballs, the skin is only one layer thick and the gleba is never powdery, but may be rubbery, spongy, slimy, tough, or rock hard; the spores are produced in minute chambers, which can be seen with a hand lens, rather than in coarse chambers, easily visible to the unaided eye as in the case of the true truffles (order Tuberales in the Ascomyceteae). These false truffles are covered with rhizomorphs, or fine, rootlike threads. They have not been tested for edibility; however, wild animals eat them with relish.

Rhodophyllaceae = *Entolomataceae*

Rhodophyllus = *Entoloma*

Rozites. (CORT—1, 1) Medium-sized, terrestrial mushroom with a parabolic to campanulate cap which may become convex or obscurely mammilate in age; stems fleshy fibrous with prominent, membranous ring; gills adnate to notched, changing from off-white to brown with lighter and darker zones, spore print dark rusty brown; base of stem often scurfy and sometimes appears to have an obscure volva or volva-like zone. *Rozites* has a dry cap which is radially wrinkled and covered with a frosty sheen when young; these features, together with the volva-like zone at the base of the stem, when present, should serve to differentiate *Rozites* from *Pholiota* and other fleshy stemmed Cortinariaceae.

Russula. (RUSS—300NA, 12) Robust, white-spored mushrooms with thick, brittle stems and attached gills. Ring and volva both absent. At maturity, the cap is often depressed, almost funnel-shaped; otherwise it is flat; it is often dry when mature, though sticky earlier, and the skin peels easily. The brittle flesh, flat or depressed dry cap with humus and debris clinging to it, and peeling characteristics make this a very easy genus to identify. Since both edible and poisonous species occur, care must be exercised in identifying species; see Chapter Four.

Russulaceae. A family characterized by brittle flesh and robust stature to which the genera *Russula* and *Lactarius* belong. Two other genera, now included in the Hymenogastraceae, probably should be transferred to this family: *Arcangeliella* which shows anatomical and biochemical affinities to *Lactarius*, and *Macowanites* which shows similar affinities to *Russula*.

Russulineae. The sub-order of the Agaricales to which the Russulaceae belong. The internal gill tissues contain sphaerocysts, or spherical cells in addition to the usual elongated, prosenchymatous cells found in other Agaricales.

Sarcosphaera. (PEZI—ca. 10, 2) Cup fungi which superficially resemble puffballs or truffles; fruiting body spherical, buried in the soil, but as it expands, it partially emerges, the skin breaks into rays, and it takes on a crown-like appearance. Species that have been tested have been declared edible and good by some mycophagists and poisonous by others.

Schizophyllaceae. Family to which the genus *Schizophyllum* belongs. Formerly included in the Agaricales, *Schizophyllum* is now placed in the Aphyllophorales by most mycologists.

Schizophyllum. (SCHI—3, 1) Small to medium-sized, wood-inhabiting shelf fungus with gills radiating out from the point of attachment of the margin to the log or stick; cap fan-shaped, spore print white. Its most distinctive characterisitic is its broad, split gills which are inrolled when dry.

Scleroderma. (SCLE—40, 1) Puffball-like, buried, or partially buried, thick skinned fungi in which the wall or skin is single layered and there is no capillitium. The gleba of the immature fruit becomes purplish or black very early, and the wall lacks the spines common in many of the *Lycoperdons* or the warts typical of *Calvatia.* At maturity, the wall splits longitudinally like the outer wall of *Astreus* to form a star-like structure and the powdery spores escape. Besides being too tough to eat, the fruits are usually bitter and some species are poisonous.

Sclerodermataceae. The family of Lycoperdales to which *Scleroderma, Tulostoma,* and *Battaraea* belong. *Astreus* is also often included in this family. Some taxonomists place the family in the Hymenogastrales, or in the Lycoperdales, and others in an order by itself, the Sclerodermatales.

Sparassis. (CLAV—5, 1) A highly branched sporocarp in which the branches are flattened or ribbon-like, giving it the appearance of a tangle of noodles or sometimes a head of cabbage, characterize this genus which is sometimes included in the Clavariaceae, or in the Thelephoraceae. Only one species is found in North America and it is edible and choice in addition to being very easily identified.

Stropharia. (STRO—30, 5) A small genus of saprophytic fungi commonly found in lawns and meadows, occasionally in woods. It is characterized by almost free gills, purple-brown to almost black spore print, and a distinct though not especially prominent ring. It is frequently confused with *Agaricus, Agrocybe, Hebeloma,* or *Psilocybe;* occasionally with *Naematoloma. Agaricus* has free gills that are usually pink when young; *Agrocybe* and *Hebeloma* have a browner spore print and usually lack a ring; *Psilocybe* has a stem or cap that stains blue or green, or else it lacks a ring. Several species are edible, though generally rated mediocre; however, caution should be exercised because some species are reported to be poisonous and there is a danger of confusion with other genera.

Strophariaceae. A rather small family of attractive mushrooms saprophytic on wood, leaf litter, or manure from herbivores. It is of very little importance to mushroom eaters, except for the negative feature that several mildly poisonous species occur. To the user of "magic mushrooms," however, this is the most important of all mushroom families. The family contains the genera *Hypholoma, Naematoloma, Psilocybe,* and *Stropharia.* *Hypholoma* and *Psilocybe* are usually combined in one genus.

Suillus. (BOLE—ca. 30NA, 11) Mostly robust, mycorrhizal mushrooms associated with conifers formerly included in the genus *Boletus* and overlapping its characteristics. The genus is described in Chapter Four. Both edible and inedible species occur, but no poisonous species are known; however, care must be taken to avoid confusion with poisonous species of *Boletus.* (Synonym: *Ixocomus;* Seg. *Boletinus*)

Thelephora (THEL—75, 0) Tough to woody bracket fungi and coral-like fungi characterized by minute (microscopically small) pores and velvety hymenium; spore print is dark reddish-brown to purplish brown. None of the species are known to be either edible or poisonous.

Thelephoraceae. A family of mostly polypore-like fungi having minute pores and dark colored spores, or with funnel shaped sporocarps growing on humus or litter. Genera include *Clavariella, Scytinopogon, Thelephora, Coniophorella, Peniophora, Aleurodiscus, Dendrothele, Vararia, Cladoderris, Skepperia,* and others. Many of these genera are placed in different families by different mycologists.

Tremella. (TREM—45, 1) Jelly fungi growing on sticks, logs, or stumps, jelly-like when moist, bone hard when dry, varying from bright yellow or orange to brown, commonly called "witch's butter." Most if not all of the species are edible and tasteless; if fried, they evaporate into nothing.

Tremellaceae. Family of jelly mushrooms to which *Calocera,*

Cerinomyces, Dacrymyces, Exidia, Phlogiotis, Pseudohydnum, and other gelatinous fungi belong. The first three are sometimes placed in a separate family and order, the Dacrymycetaceae and Dacrymycetales. The family is closely related to the Auriculariaceae.

Tremellales. The order to which the Tremellaceae, the jelly fungi, belongs. It is closely related to and sometimes united with the Auriculariales.

Tricholoma. (TRIC—140, 2) Medium to large terrestrial fungi, probably mycorrhizal with pine and other trees, fruiting primarily in cold weather, and characterized by the almost free, light colored gills, white spore print, and fleshy fibrous stem. Veil is absent or rudimentary; volva is absent. It is easily distinguished from *Entoloma* and *Hebeloma* by spore color and from *Collybia* and *Russula* by its thick but not brittle and not cartilaginous stem. Some very choice, edible species occur, but there are also some poisonous species in the genus, so caution is advised when identifying them. No *Tricholoma* should be eaten until you have gained considerable experience with the genus.

Tricholomataceae. A large family of white spored mushrooms containing both edible and poisonous species; it differs from the Amanitaceae in having no volva and in usually having attached gills, from the Russulaceae in stem characteristics, lacking the brittle stems and flesh of the *Russulas* and *Lactarii,* from the Hygrophoracease in not having waxy gills, from the Cantharellaceae in having gills rather than veins, and from the other gill mushrooms in spore print color. Because of the large number of species and genera, the family is divided into tribes as follows: (1) Biannularieae with *Armillaria* and *Biannularia;* (2) Clitocybeae with *Clitocybe, Laccaria, Omphalina, Omphalotus, Tricholoma,* and *Tricholomopsis;* (3) Collybieae with *Collybia* and *Marasmiellus;* (4) Cystodermateae with *Cystoderma, Dissoderma,* and *Ripartitella;* (5) Leucopaxilleae with *Cantharellula, Leucopaxillus,* and *Porpolma;* (6) Lyophylleae with *Asterophora, Calocybe,* and *Lyophyllum;* (7) Marasmieae with *Crinipellis, Marasmius,* and *Strobilurus;* (8) Myceneae with *Delicatula, Mycena,* and *Xeromphalina;* (9) Panelleae with *Panellus* and *Tectella;* (10) Pleuroteae with *Geopetalum,*

Lentinus, Phyllotopsis, and *Pleurotus;* (11) Pseudohiatuleae with *Cryptotrama, Flammulina,* and *Pseudohiatula;* (12) Resupinateae with *Hohenbuehelia* and *Resupinatus;* and (13) Rhodoteae with *Rhodotus* and *Termitomyces.*

Tubaria. (CORT—10, 2) Very common little brown mushrooms similar in appearance to *Galerina* but with decurrent gills and no annulus. Edibility is unknown but their relationship to *Galerina* suggests caution; do not taste test these or other related LBM's.

Tuber. (TUBE—50, 0) Subterranean ascomycetes consisting of chambered spheres. There are at least six species of *Tuber* in North America; edibility unknown.

Tuberaceae. The family to which *Tuber* and other truffles belong. Superficially, these underground ascomycetes resemble puffballs; dissection reveals numerous small, but macroscopic, chambers in which the spores are produced. The family contains about 16 genera including *Balsamia, Choiromyces, Hydnotria, Pachyphloeus, Piersonia,* and *Tuber.*

Tuberales. Small to medium-sized underground mushrooms; the ascocarps are more or less globose or irregularly warty, lobed or bowl-shaped; the interior is marbled with channels, veins, or cavities; the fruits are fleshy or hard at maturity. Commonly called *Truffles,* these are considered the choicest of all mushrooms by most mycophagists; they are certainly the most expensive. Their adaptation for dissemination is a strong pleasant odor which attracts ground squirrels, deer, and other animals which eat them and spread the spores. Goats, dogs, and pigs are often trained to hunt for them. The order contains four families, the Tuberaceae (or Eutuberaceae), the Geneaceae, the Elaphomycetaceae, and the Terfeziaceae; however, the last two are often classified with other ascomycetes. When the sporocarps are dissected, the channels along which the spores are produced make identification certain. Very little is known about the edibility of North American species, most of which are found in the oak woods of California and Oregon.

Verpa. (HELV—5, 1) Morel-like mushrooms in which the pits, if present, are elongated rather than squarish as in *Morchella;* the caps are typically conical and the margin is free from the white, hollow stem. *Verpa* species are edible, but, like other Helvellaceae, should never be eaten raw.

Volvariaceae. Small to medium-sized mushrooms with pink or reddish spore print, a central stem, and gills free at maturity. The other family (Entolomataceae) with pink spores has attached gills and angular spores: the spores of Volvariaceae are smooth. Of the three genera in this family, *Volvariella* has a volva but no ring, *Chameota* has a ring but no volva, and *Pluteus* has neither ring nor volva. The family is usually regarded as being closely related to the Amanitaceae and the Entolomataceae, but significant anatomical differences suggest that the relationship is not as close as has been believed.

Volvariella. (VOLV—ca. 30, 2) Small to medium-sized fungi found on wood or rich soil, characterized by free gills and reddish spore print. Except for spore color, *Volvariella* resembles *Amanita* and *Agaricus,* and in the tropics, replaces *Agaricus* as the principal mushrooms of commerce. Many of the species are edible and choice; however, care must be exercised to distinguish between *Volvariella,* on the one hand, and *Amanita* and *Entoloma,* on the other, before eating any of these mushrooms.

glossary

acetocarmine, n. A widely employed biological dye commonly used to stain chromosomes and other structures containing nucleic acids.

adnate, adj. Having the gills attached directly to and at right angles to the stem.

adnexed, adj. Having the gills attached only to the apex of the stem so that the gills are almost free from the stem.

alga, n. Any autotrophic aquatic plant, other than a moss, liverwort, or vascular plant, usually microscopic, but including the giant kelps and other seaweeds. (pl. algae)

Amanita, n. A genus of mushrooms characterized by white spore print, presence of both annulus and volva, and free gills. Many of the species are deadly poisonous.

amanitin, n. A protoplasmic toxin found in species of *Amanita, Galerina,* and some other mushrooms.

amino acid, n. An organic compound characterized by the presence of an amine (NH_2) group and a carboxyl (COOH) group; amino acids are the basic buildings blocks of which proteins are made up.

amorphous, adj. Without any distinctive shape or form.

amyloid, adj. In reference to spores, staining blue, violet, or bluish gray in Melzer's or Gram's iodine solutions due to the presence of amylose or starch.

angiosperm, n. Any vascular plant which produces flowers, and hence has seeds enclosed in a ripened ovary or fruit; woody angiosperms are commonly called hardwoods.

annulus, n. A ring of tissue surrounding the stipe or stem of a mushroom formed from the remnants of the inner or partial veil; commonly called a ring.

antiphallin serum, n. A serum reportedly being used in France, but not available in the United States, which counteracts amanitin or phallin.

apex, n. The tip or upper end of a sporocarp or other structure.

apothecium, n. A spore fruit, or ascocarp, having a disk or cuplike shape with spores produced on its upper surface in small sacs or asci. (pl. apothecia)

appendiculate, adj. Referring to a sporocarp cap having ragged edges with bits of cap tissue hanging from the margin.

ascocarp, n. A sporocarp in which the spores, usually eight in number, are enclosed in small sacs or asci.

ascomycete, n. A sac fungus, or fungus belonging to the class Ascomyceteae.

ascospore, n. A reproductive structure or spore produced when an ascus mother cell undergoes meiosis; the meiospore of the ascomycetes.

ascus, n. The small sac in which the meiospores in plants of the class Ascomyceteae are contained. (pl. asci)

autotrophic, adj. Having the ability to manufacture sugar and other organic substances by means of photosynthesis.

basidiocarp, n. The sporocarp of the Basidiomyceteae, the class of plants to which most mushrooms belong. The meiospores are typically produced on the undersurface of a relatively large cap or pileus, with four spores produced on each club shaped structure or basidium.

basidiomycete, n. A fungus of the class Basidiomyceteae in which the meiospores are typically produced on club shaped structures called basidia.

basidiospore, n. A meiospore produced on a club shaped structure called a basidum located on or within a basidiocarp.

basidium, n. A club shaped structure on the gills or in the pores or other structure of the sporocarps on the Basidiomycopsida. (pl. basidia)

bioluminescence, n. The emission of visible light by a living organism.

bolete, n. A mushroom belonging to the genera *Boletus* or *Suillus* or any of the segregate genera separated from *Boletus.*

boletiod, adj. Spindle shaped, referring to spores.

bracket fungus, n. A fungus which grows on logs, stumps, or tree trunks, characterized by shelflike, usually woody, sporocarps.

button, n. A small, immature mushroom still enclosed in the universal veil.

campanulate, adj. Bell-like in shape.

cartilaginous, adj. Having a thin, stringy, often tough stem, usually less than 5 mm. in diameter, in contrast to a firm, fleshy or brittle, thick stem.

cellulose, n. A polymer of glucose or other monosaccharides [$(C_6H_{10}O_5)n$] which makes up about 70% of the matter in wood, and of which the primary cell walls of most plants is produced.

cep, n. A common name for the king bolete, *Boletus edulis.*

cespitose, adj. Tufted or growing in tufts, typically with short stems which may be fused together at the base.

chlorpromazine, n. A grayish, crystalline drug ($C_{17}H_{19}ClN_2S$) used as a sedative and/or to prevent or relieve nausea.

circa, adv. Approximately. (abbrev. ca.)

clavate, adj. Club shaped.

club fungus, n. A basidiomycete, so called because the spores are typically borne on minute club-shaped structures within or on the surface of a sporocarp or spore fruit. Most mushrooms are club fungi; others are sac fungi or ascomycetes.

columella, n. A column or vein of sterile tissue extending through the gleba or spore-bearing tissue of many puffball-like mushrooms such as some of the Phallaceae.

complex, n. A group of organisms that are difficult to distinguish from each other, being similar in a number of ways to one another, and usually closely related to each other, such as the *Amanita phalloides* complex and the *Morchella esculenta* complex.

concave, adj. Referring to a surface which is depressed in the center.

concentric, adj. Referring to a series of circles of different diameters all having the same center.

conic, adj. Shaped like a cone, *viz.,* having a circular bottom and with sides that taper evenly to a point.

conk, n. A hard, woody, usually perennial basidiocarp, growing on tree trunks, stumps, or logs.

convex, adj. Referring to a disk-like surface which gradually rises toward the center.

convoluted, adj. Having twisted or distorted ridges or wrinkles.

convolution, n. One of the twisted ridges or wrinkles on the sporocarps of some Helvellaceae or other mushrooms.

cordate, adj. Shaped like a heart, specifically a valentine heart, being rounded and having an indentation at the base and tapering to a point at the apex.

cortina, n. A web-like remnant of the universal veil resembling the cortina or veil worn by women in some cultures.

coral, adj. Referring to erect, usually sparsely branched mushrooms, having the general appearance of marine coral.

couplet, n. One of a pair, or sometimes set of three or more, contrasting statements in a biological key with which an unknown specimen is compared in the process of identification.

crenate, adj. Having rounded projections, or scalloping, along the margin of the cap.

crenulate, adj. Minutely crenate, or minutely scalloped.

crisped, adj. Referring to the gills or the cap margins, being crinkled along the edge.

cross veins, n. Veins that join one primary vein to another, at right angles to both, as in the chanterelles.

crustose, adj. Growing like a thin crust on the soil or other substrate surface.

cuticle, n. The non-cellular layer of material on the surface of the caps of some species of mushrooms.

cysteine, n. A crystalline, sulfer-containing amino acid having the empirical formula, $C_2H_4SNH_2COOH$.

decomposer organism, n. An organism especially adapted to breaking organic compounds down into carbon dioxide, water, and inorganic mineral substances.

deciduous, adj. Losing its leaves, or other appendages, in the autumn season.

decurrent, adj. Referring to gills that arc downward as they reach the stem and are attached to a long portion of the stem.

deliquesce, v. To become liquid gradually.

dicaryotic, adj. Having two haploid nuclei in the same cell, which then usually behaves genetically like a diploid cell.

dichotomously branched, adj. Referring to gills or stems that repeatedly fork into two equal branches.

disc, n. A rounded, flat structure. (Also spelled disk.)

disulfiram, n. A harmless drug which causes nausea when taken with alcohol and therefore used in treating alcoholism.

duff, n. The dead and partially decomposed matter on the soil surface in forests, also called litter.

eccentric, adj. Set with its axis or support off center, thus, any mushroom in which the stem is not attached to the center of the cap.

ellipsoid, adj. A three dimensional figure, such as a spore, in which the longitudinal planes have the shape of an ellipse or symmetrical closed curve with one axis longer than the other.

emetic, n. A substance which induces vomiting.

entire, adj. Referring to sporocarp margins, being smooth and continuous without serrations, wrinkles, or indentations.

enzyme, n. An organic catalyst, or substance which speeds up the rate of a chemical reaction without being permanently altered itself, specifically, any protein having this ability.

epidermis, n. The outermost layer or layers of cells covering the cap or stem of a mushroom; the "peeling."

fairy ring, n. A naturally occurring circle of fruiting bodies of any mushroom.

farinaceous, adj. Having the odor of newly milled wheat or the texture of flour.

fascicle, n. Two or more sporocarps or other structures arising from a common point and attached at the base to each other.

fatal five, n. A common name applied to a group of five species complexes containing some of the most poisonous of all mushrooms: The *Amanita phalloides* complex, the *Entoloma lividum* complex, the *Galerina venenata* complex, the *Amanita muscaria* complex, and the *Gyromitra esculenta* complex.

fibrillose, adj. Covered with appressed hairs or threads (fibrils) more or less evenly disposed.

fibrous, adj. Made up of elongated cells called fibers, hence any firm to tough stringy tissue.

fleshy fibrous, adj. Having a relatively thick stem, usually greater than 5 mm. in diameter, made up of short fibers which give it a firm, fleshy consistency, as in the common cultivated mushroom, in contrast to the thin, stringy, cartilaginous stems of the *Galerinas* or the thick, brittle stems of the *Russulas.*

fluted, adj. With longitudinal ridges, as in the stems of some mushrooms.

foolproof four, n. A common name applied to four species complexes of edible mushrooms which are so easy to identify that essentially no risk of accidentally eating a poisonous species exists. These are the morels, the sulfur polypore, the shaggy mane and the puffballs.

free, adj. A term used in reference to gills that are not attached to the stem at all. Careful examination is essential to distinguish between free and adnexed gills.

fruiting body, n. The sporocarp of a mushroom; the portion that is commonly called mushroom and within or upon which the spores are produced.

fungus, n. Common name for any living organism which is heterotrophic but more plant-like than animal-like in its chemical compostion, life cycle, and general structure. Although not able to synthesize sugars from carbon dioxide and water, most fungi are able to synthesize amino acids and other compounds from inorganic substances. (pl. fungi)

funiculus, n. In the Nudulariaceae, or bird's nest fungi, a small cord which is attached to the peridioles, or "eggs."

funnel, n. A hollow structure with a broad, round apex tapering to a base of small diameter.

Galerina, n. A genus of small, brown mushrooms having mammillate to conic or convex caps and rough, broadly ovate, brown spores, and including some very poisonous species.

gastrointestinal irritant, n. A group of mushroom toxins which cause indigestion, diarrhea, and other intestinal disturbances. Some of these poisons are sometimes fatal.

gelatinous, adj. Viscous, having the consistency of gelatin; in mushrooms, referring to how a dry or slightly moist cap feels to the touch.

genus, n. A group of closely related species of plants or animals especially if they are so closely related that some exchange of genetic matter is conceivable among them. The name of the genus to which a species belongs is the first part of the scientific name of that species.

gill, n. A vertical flat plate on the undersurface of many mushroom caps upon which the spores are borne.

glabrous, adj. Having a smooth surface, specifically having a surface devoid of hairs, glands, or remnants of the universal veil; bald.

glandular, adj. Having minute pores, usually on the stems, which secrete a resinous or dark colored material causing the stem to become spotted.

gleba, n. The sporogenous tissue in puffballs and related mushrooms; it may be dry or slimy and often fills the interior of the sporocarp with a dark-colored spore mass at maturity.

glutinous, adj. Covered with a slimy to sticky layer.

gregarious, adj. Growing close together in large groups but not clustered or attached to each other.

gymnocarpous, adj. Referring to sporocarp development in which the sporocarps are naked, *viz.* have no sterile layers of tissue enclosing the sporocarps themselves.

gymnosperm, n. A seed plant, such as the pines and the cycads, in which the seeds are borne on the scales of a strobilis or cone instead of within an enclosed pericarp or fruit; gymnosperm trees are commonly called softwoods.

gyromitrin, n. A volatile, heat labile, powerful toxin found in many members of the Helvellaceae and sometimes responsible for deaths, especially when these mushrooms have been eaten raw.

hemodialysis, n. Selective diffusion of hemoglobin.

herbarium, n. A library or collection of preserved plants which can be used to aid in identification of unknown specimens by comparison to the identified specimens in the collection.

heterogeneous, adj. Pertaining to a mixture; not uniform in cell composition or tissue structure.

heterotrophic, adj. Not capable of producing primary food molecules, such as sugars, by means of photosynthesis.

humus, n. Organic matter which has been decomposed to the extent that cell structure is no longer apparent.

hymenium, n. The spore producing layer in mushrooms and other fungi.

hypha, n. A thread-like filament, made up of cells arranged end to end, which is usually branched but may be unbranched, and which with other like filaments make up the mycelium or vegetative part of the mushroom. (pl. hyphae)

ibotenic acid, n. A hallucinogenic drug found in *Amanita muscaria* and its relatives, chemically interconvertible with muscimol.

inky cap, n. Any of a group of mushrooms of the genus *Coprinus*, in which the gills and then the cap and stem, deliquesce, or autodigest, into a black, inky mass of liquid and spores.

key, n. A device consisting of a series of couplets, each couplet being composed of two or more contrasting statements, employed by biologists in identifying unknown specimens. The specimen is compared with each set of statements until, through the process of elimination, the correct name is reached.

knobby, adj. Having an enlarged apex.

KOH, n. Potassium hydroxide, used to recognize some chemical compounds often present in mushrooms and thus aid in their identification; frequently used as a mounting medium for mushroom spores.

larva, n. The first stage in the life cycle of an insect after the egg has hatched, commonly called a "worm." (pl. larvae)

latex, n. A juice, milky or colored, which is exuded when a mushroom is injured.

lead, n. In a biological key, one of a set of contrasting statements used in identifying unknown species; each couplet in the key consists of two or sometimes more, leads.

lignicolous, adj. Growing on logs or stumps or any material with a high lignin content.

lignin, n. A polymer of shikimic acid making up about 25% of the material in wood and providing hardness, elasticity, and strength to wood.

litter, n. The undecomposed organic matter on the soil surface consisting primarily of dead leaves and small twigs.

mammillate, adj. Having nipples or small protuberances like nipples; hence, any mushroom cap which has the rounded shape of a breast with an umbo or nipple at or near the center.

margin, n. The edge of a mushroom cap; the margin may be entire, crenulate, serrate, inrolled, etc., and this characteristic may be useful in its identification.

membranous, adj. Thin, having the appearance of paper or other thin material.

metabolic, adj. Referring to an effect on the metabolism, or the physical and chemical processes that occur in cells.

methionine, n. A sulfur containing amino acid, $C_4H_8SNH_2COOH$.

morel, n. The common name of any member of the genus *Morchella,* especially *M. esculenta* and *M. deliciosa,* which are among the most choice of all mushrooms and included in the Foolproof Four.

muscarine, n. A mushroom toxin found in *Amanita muscaria* and some other mushrooms, the ingestion of which can be fatal.

muscimol, n. A hallucinogenic toxin found in some *Amanitas;* it is interconvertable to ibotenic acid.

mushroom, n. Any fleshy fungus, edible or poisonous, having a sporocarp that is large enough that it can conceivably be eaten.

mycelium, n. The vegetative part of a mushroom, usually perennial and growing at the interface between soil and litter; made up of branched filaments called hyphae.

mycophagy, n. The act or practice of eating mushrooms.

mycorrhiza, n. A root-like structure commonly found on naturally growing vascular plants consisting of vascular plant tissue and fungal hyphae intimately associated with each other and usually mutually beneficial to each other.

navel, n. A depression in the middle of the abdomen left as a scar after separation from the umbilical cord; hence, any structure in mushrooms or other plants that resembles such a scar.

nipple, n. A protuberance on the upper surface of a mushroom cap which is centrally located giving the appearance of a mammalian nipple.

notched, adj. Referring to gills in which a small notch occurs at the point of attachment to the stem; between adnate and adnexed in gill attachment.

oblique, adj. Slanting or inclined as an oblique annulus.

ocher, adj. A reddish brown color, also called faded rose, having more yellow in it than cinnamon.

olivaceous, adj. Being the color of a ripe olive, a dull greenish brown.

operculum, n. The lid or flap covering an opening at the apex of an ascus; the opening at the apex of some puffballs.

pallid, adj. Pale in color, off-white.

pantherin, n. A very powerful mushroom toxin found in some species of *Amanita,* especially *A. pantherina,* which has caused some deaths among mushroom eaters.

parasite, n. Any plant or animal which lives on or in another organism from which it obtains its nourishment.

parboil, v. To boil for a specified length of time, usually five minutes, and then discard the water, in order to eliminate poisonous substances, prior to preparing a mushroom in the usual way.

partial veil, n. The inner membrane in the young sporocarp which covers the gill or pore layer; as the mushroom matures remnants of the partial veil may persist as an annulus or ring.

pellis, n. A thin skin covering the cap of some mushrooms.

peridiole, n. In the Nidulariaceae, the inner chambers of the sporocarp in which the spores are produced; the "eggs" of a birds' nest fungus.

perithecium, n. A closed, flask-shaped sporocarp containing asci and ascospores, differing from an apothecium in its smaller size and its flask-like appearance as opposed to an open disk.

persistent, adj. An annulus, or other structure, that remains intact on the stem of the mushroom until the sporocarp is completely mature.

phallin, n. A very powerful toxin found in the *Amanita phaloides* complex of mushrooms, also known as amanitin.

pileus, n. The cap of the fruiting body of a mushroom.

pitted, adj. A sporocarp which has square or oblong depressions covering the cap with distinct ridges separating them.

plane, adj. Referring to a mushroom cap that is essentially flat.

polypore, n. Any mushroom in which the undersurface of the cap is made up of minute tubes or pores forming a tough, thin pore layer attached firmly to the cap. Polypores are frequently woody in texture; few if any are poisonous, but most species are too tough and woody or too bitter to be edible.

pore, n. A minute opening by which spores or other matter may be exuded from a sporocarp or other structure.

prosenchymatous, adj. A tissue which is obviously made up of hyphae or filaments and in which the filamentous nature of the tissue is apparent.

protoplasmic toxin, n. Any toxin which does its damage by dissolving or digesting the cell contents or intracellular matter.

pseudorhiza, n. In some mushrooms, the tapered base of the sporocarp, which resembles a taproot of a seed plant.

psilocybin, n. One of several hallucinogenic toxins found in mushrooms.

psilocin, n. A hallucinogenic toxin found in some mushrooms.

ptomaine, n. Any organic base or alkaloid produced by bacterial decomposition of proteins or other nitrogenous material. Some ptomaines may be poisonous, but most are harmless; however, the bacteria which produce the ptomaines often produce very powerful toxins which can accumulate in the decomposed mushroom, meat, or other proteinaceous matter.

pubescent, adj. Covered with short hairs.

puffball, n. A mushroom of the family Lycoperdaceae characterized by the entire contents of the sporocarp developing into spores which may escape through a bellows action or by fragmentation of the entire sporocarp, depending on species. Puffballs are so abundant, so tasty, and so easily recognized that they are included in the Foolproof Four.

reticulate, adj. Having a net-like appearance.

rhizine, n. A differentiated, multicellular structure, common in the lichens and present in some mushrooms, which anchors the plant to the substrate, and superficially resembles the roots of flowering plants.

rhizomorph, n. In the "false truffles," family Hymenogastraceae, the sporocarp is often covered by fine, rootlike threads, called rhizomorphs.

rind, n. The skin or epidermis on a mushroom cap.

ring, n. An annulus; a ring of tissue formed from remnants of the inner or partial veil.

rosette, n. A rose-like structure made up of overlapping caps of mushrooms having short stems attached marginally.

sac fungus, n. Any fungus in which the meiospores are produced within a sac or ascus, hence any ascomycete.

saprophyte, n. An organism which lives on the dead organic matter in the soil or other substratum.

scale, n. A dry, often hard structure, formed from torn bits of veil tissue or cuticle; usually the scales have some pattern of dispersal.

scurfy, adj. Rough, usually as the result of numerous small scales or glandular dots.

seceding, adj. Referring to a gill attachment which started out as adnexed but in the mature sporocarp appears to be free.

septate, adj. Having cross walls present, separating the protoplasm of the mushroom hyphae into distinct cells.

serrate. adj. Having sawtooth-like indentations on the edges of the gills or other structures.

serum, n. The liquid portion of blood that remains after the red and white blood cells and the fibrinogen have been removed, usually by centrifugation; the antibodies, including antitoxins, are included in the serum, which can be used, therefore, to eliminate toxins from the body.

shaggy mane, n. A mushroom with a narrowly parabolic cap and gills which deliquesce; one of the Foolproof Four.

shelf fungus, n. A fungus, usually a polypore, which is attached by its margin to a tree trunk, log, or stump and thus resembles a shelf.

slimy, adj. Having a wet, mucous-like, more or less slick substance on the upper surface of the cap.

slippery jack, n. Any one of several species of *Boletus* which has a slimy coating on the spore fruit, thus giving it a slippery feeling.

species, n. The basic unit of taxonomy, consisting of all the populations of a kind of plant capable of interbreeding to produce fertile offspring. The species name consists of two parts, the name of the genus to which it belongs and its own species epithet.

species epithet, n. The second part of a species scientific name.

sphaerocyst, n. Large, bubble-shaped hyphal cells which commonly occur in the sporocarps of the Russulaceae.

spheroid, adj. Referring to spores, resembling spheres and hence round in cross-section.

spindle shaped, adj. In reference to spores, resembling a spindle; having a larger diameter at the center and tapering to two poles.

spine, n. Small, slender, pointed protuberances on spores or on the undersurface of some mushrooms.

spore, n. (1) A reproductive structure resulting from meiosis, and the beginning of the haploid stage of the life cycle; a meiospore. (2) An asexual spore having the same number of chromosomes as the cell from which it was produced, common in some fungi but rare in mushrooms.

spore fruit, n. A sporocarp; a large structure containing meiospores and commonly called a mushroom.

spore print, n. A mass of spores deposited on a piece of paper by placing a sporocarp hymenium side down and covering with a tumbler; an aid in observing spore color and shape to help in the identification of a specimen.

sporocarp, n. The fruiting body or reproductive structure of a mushroom in which the spores are produced.

squamule, n. Small, usually overlapping scales.

stalk, n. The "stem" of the mushroom, also called a "stipe."

stipe, n. A stem-like structure commonly observed in large seaweeds such as the kelps; hence, the stem of the mushroom.

striate, adj. Having radiating markings on the upper surface of the cap.

striation, n. A marking radiating out from the center of the upper surface of the cap of a mushroom.

substrate, n. The material on which a mushroom grows, such as soil, lignin, litter, etc.

sulfur polypore, n. One of the Foolproof Four; a species of mushroom characterized by overlapping, yellow or orange sporocarps with pores on the undersurface.

symbiosis, n. A relationship between two species in which each is benefited by the association, as in the case of most mycorrhizal relationships in which the tree and the mushroom both benefit.

synonym, n. An alternate scientific name; many species of fungi are known by two scientific names as the result of differences of opinion as to how the species should be classified.

tacky, adj. Having a sticky substance on the upper surface of the cap as in many boletes.

taxon, n. A taxonomic group or entity of any rank.

thioctic acid, n. A hallucinogenic substance found in some mushrooms.

toadstool, n. (1) Any poisonous mushroom; hence a term without any botanical significance since both poisonous and edible species are found in most botanical families. (2) A common name for *Amanita muscaria,* a common poisonous mushroom.

toothed mushroom, n. A member of the Hydnaceae in which the spore bearing tissue consists of tooth-like projections.

translucent, adj. Allowing light to pass through in such a way that a clear image is not seen, therefore, not transparent.

truffle, n. Any mushroom of the order Tuberales, characterized by a more or less spheroidal form, a gleba differentiated into distinct chambers, and subterranean habit; these are highly prized, rare, and hence expensive mushrooms, generally imported from France or Italy.

umbilicate, adj. Having the center of the cap depressed with a protuberance or umbo in the center of the depression.

umbo, n. A protuberance on the upper surface of a sporocarp cap resembling the boss on a knight's shield.

undulating, adj. Having a wavy pattern, as on the margin of a sporocarp cap or the edge of the gills of a mushroom.

universal veil, n. A membranous material which covers the entire sporocarp as it first emerges; it then ruptures as the sporocarp grows and its remnants may form patches or warts on the upper surface of the cap, a volva or cup at the lower end of the stem, or a cortina.

vegetative, adj. The non-reproductive portion of a plant.

veil, n. A membranous material enclosing a sporocarp or part of one.

vinaceous, adj. Wine colored; reddish.

viscid, adj. Sticky to the touch.

volatile, adj. Evaporating at relatively low temperatures.

volva, n. Usually a cup-like structure at the base of the stem of a mushroom, which may be reduced to markings of various kinds, formed from remnants of the universal veil.

wart, n. A patch of material on the upper surface of a cap that originated from part of the torn universal veil.

waxy, adj. In some mushrooms, having a waxy material on the cap or the gills giving them a waxy sheen and leaving a thin layer of wax on the fingers when the gills or cap is rubbed.

zygote, n. A cell produced by the fusion of two gametes and having, therefore, the diploid—or in many fungi, the dicaryotic—number of chromosomes.

index
(see also glossary and list of families and genera)